FREDERICK

Seeking communion with the living God

first edition

author's edition
Maringá (PR)
April/2021

ISBN: 978-65-00-20662-3 (e-book):
ISBN: 978-65-00-20658-6 (printed version):

Acquire other titles of the Author through the websites (www.amazon and https://clubedeautores.com.br)

Contact me and give your opinion:
walterkrusebr@hotmail.com

"Behold, I stand at the door and knock. If anyone hears my voice and opens the door, I will come into his house and dine with him, and he with me" (BTE, Jesus Christ, Re 3:20).

To my beloved son, David Frederick Kruse, who helped me greatly in this endeavor;

to my beloved sister, Mirian, for her encouragement and affection.

SUMMARY

1 *Sin and communion with God*

The Bible teaches that God desired to complete the creation of the visible world in a spectacular way, forming his masterpiece: the human being.[1]

God created Man in his own image and likeness, as the book of Genesis 1:26-27 tells us, breathing a breath of life into his nostrils.[2][3]

Endowed with a much more complex and perfect organism - compared to other beings, Man was created with the ability to reason and express himself completely.

He was the only being of the visible world who had the privilege of receiving the Lord's visit at the end of each day's evening. The Bible does not report details of this encounter, but it was certainly a wonderful moment of sharing and communion surrounded by an atmosphere of goodness, joy and light.

The human being belongs to a unique category among the living beings, conscious of himself and of the reality that surrounds him, able to live in society, to be emotional, to reason and to make his choices, began to exercise dominion over the Earth as predicted in the Bible. [4]

It is to use very poor vocabulary, not to say inaccurate, to call the human being "rational animal". Jesus taught us that, for God, human beings are much more important than animals, and only the first can be saved from death and commune with God. The horizon of life for the human being does not end with death. [5]

If the destiny of men were that of animals, it would be better to take advantage of everything that life offers us as the Apostle Paul argued (1 Corinthians 15:32). [6]

Originally, God desired that human beings should live eternally, enjoying daily communion with God and a comfortable and pleasurable life.

The first men had a more perfect constitution and were longer-lived, until God limited their age to 120 years, which is the limit also found by science to human life in conditions close to ideals. [7]

The disobedience of the human being, however, brought consequences such as the limitation of his days here on earth and the dependence on work for his own sustenance.

Although we can no longer live in conditions prior to the fall of Man, God desires to establish close fellowship with us.

God's desire is that every human being should have a blessed earthly life and that his spirit, after earthly death, should live eternally with him in his Kingdom. In the 1st Epistle of Timothy, chapter 2, verses 3 and 4, we read, "Behold, it is good and acceptable in the sight of God our Saviour, who willeth that all men should be saved, and come to the knowledge of the truth."

It is out of human understanding, the life of happiness and pleasure that awaits the redeemed in the heavenly kingdom. When God created man, He endowed him with the chemical and hormonal processes that regulate his sensations of pleasure, which are nothing more than a timid and small show of what is reserved for the elect of God.

Jesus teaches that "the righteous will shine like the sun in the kingdom of their Father" (Matthew 13:43). Paul exclaims,

"As it is written, what the eyes have not seen, the ears have not heard, and the heart of man hath not perceived, that God hath prepared for them that love him" (1 Corinthians 2:9).[8]

Fellowship with God happens when we know the truth and desire that relationship above all else.

Jesus compared the kingdom of heaven to a pearl of great value that, found by a collector, sells everything he has to acquire it (Matthew 13:45-46). [9]

The relationship with God is not only a reserve of daily time for reading the Word and prayer, but rather means placing life in the context of the Bible.

One of the wonderful ways the Holy Spirit converses with us is in projecting into the mind of Bible verses that we remember when facing a problem. The Holy Spirit commonly speaks to us through the Word and whoever desires to have a relationship with God needs to hear the Word ("faith comes from preaching, and preaching is the announcement of the word of Christ," Romans 10:17, BTE).

If you sincerely desire to seek God, you have already taken a fundamental step in the right direction, towards a new life full of meaning, noble goals and hope, except for the condemnation that will be destined for those who have lived without God and who will spend eternity in absolute darkness, deprived of the loving and luminous atmosphere provided by the divine presence.

God is good and just when He warns us of the final judgment, because in this way He is giving the opportunity for many to attain salvation and His will is for all to obtain it.

Is God being righteous with us when he puts the choice between life and death before us? I'm sure you do! In the foreground, if we put in these terms the discussion, we cannot lose sight of the fact that the full application of the righteousness of God, which is highly severe and founded on personal merit, would lead to the condemnation of all.

Through Jesus, we can obtain salvation by grace, not by works, so that no one can boast on the basis of his own efforts.

We cannot, however, be neutral in the Christian life and crave the communion of God. We cannot indulge the sinful life and expect God's acceptance. The Bible warns that it is about to regurgitate those who are lukewarm, that is, those who are neither hot nor cold. There is no "half-Christian".[11]

Divine judgment is a theme of which Jesus made recurring use, recommending that we should be prepared, because that time will come suddenly and will find many people unprepared. Jesus stated that only God the Father knows the day and hour of the end times, not revealing them to His own Son or to angels (Matthew 24:36).[12][13]

All the gospels contain the prophecy of Jesus as to the beginning of sorrows, which will precede the consummation of the century, that is, the end of time. Jesus foretold that the "beginning of sorrows" will consist in the appearance of false messiahs, the outbreak of wars and rumors of them, the great famine and earthquakes everywhere, the persecution of Christians, the cooling of love and the proclamation of the Gospel to all nations (Matthew 24:3-14). [14][15]

These events are a reality today, and they must happen more and more frequently until the end of time.

The great evangelistic campaigns and the penetration of the Bible, the most published book in the world, have, as a result, a great diffusion of the Gospel in our days, missing its most effective proclamation in the Arab countries, where the Muslim religion prevails, in Asia and in the Israeli nation. In Israel, the official religion is Judaism, and Jews who wish to live in Israel must declare that they follow Judaism. Israel also hinders the entry of Christian religious in the country, creating bureaucratic obstacles, as reported by the newspaper Gazeta do Povo, from Curitiba (PR), dated 15.04.2004.[16]

We can see that the time of the end is approaching. The twentieth century witnessed the bloodiest wars in the world's history (1st and 2nd World Wars), which resulted in more than 23,000,000 military losses, a figure that must be added: 1st) to the 24,000,000 military disappeared and imprisoned; 2nd) about half the sum of those figures (23,5 million) relating to losses occurring outside the battlefield. About 6 million Jews were also killed in the Second World War. In the 20th century, there were still other minor wars (Falklands, Iran-Iraq, Kuwait, Bosnia, Afghanistan, Vietnam, Korea, etc.)[17]

As far as the Jewish holocaust of the Second World War is concerned, it is curious that Germany was the country that, before the Austrian Adolf Hitler's government, welcomed the Jews best, providing them with favourable conditions for a vigorous cultural and commercial development. As Richard Z. Chesnoff writes, although the Jewish population accounted for only 1% of the German population, Jews accounted for about 5% of writers, theatre personalities and journalists; 10% of doctors and dentists; 16% of lawyers; 17% of bankers (1929); 25% of retail store owners and 79% of department store owners.[18]

Returning to the subject of judgment, the Christian cannot doubt that God's desire is for everyone to find salvation and Jesus did not come to condemn but to save many by his mercy. They are the people who condemn themselves by their words and actions, as Jesus warned when saying: "By your words you will be justified and by your words you will be condemned." We are condemning ourselves when we turn our backs on Him or when we are indifferent to the plan of divine salvation and the consequence of that attitude is death, or the perpetual estrangement from God. This will provoke, in the words of Jesus, weeping and gnashing of teeth. We can assume that the doomed souls will come to their senses, realizing that they have squandered all opportunities to turn to God and that their situation has no return.[19][20]

We come to a point of maturity, when we understand the finitude of life. In the course of it, man has every opportunity to accept God's plan. After all, the Bible is the most widely read book in the world and Christianity has been widely spread throughout the world. Christ's message seems so forceful and so revealing about God that it challenges us to make a decision to accept it or to refute it. In this way, no one can be excused for his sins, on the pretext of ignoring God and his message as the apostle Paul maintains in Romans 1:19-21. [21][22]

After earthly death, there will be the final judgment that will separate the saved, who will share with God eternal life, and the unsaved, who will live completely apart from God, in suffering and deep remorse.

Between God's desire to redeem all and the realization of this plan, there is a great and terrible obstacle. This obstacle can be compared, figuratively, to an existing abyss between God and man and the name of this villain is sin. Simply put, God abhors sin by the harmful consequences of relationship with his beloved creature, since one cannot establish communion between the Holy and the unclean.[23]

Something is missing in our natural constitution that drives us to sin. Although our conscience is wrong, our eyes relish the taste of sin. tell us that

The forceful language of the Bible, which does not use half-words, records that Man becomes a "slave" to sin. We're talking about the natural man or the "old man".[24][25]

What is sin, after all? Often it appears in the form of something momentarily pleasurable. Having lustful desire - not just appreciating feminine beauty - can seem harmless and even natural. It seems tempting to appropriate something that interests us and may not be valuable, like a pretty pen, when we have the opportunity to swipe it without anyone seeing. Other times, sin arises as an act that causes harm to another person as a false testimony, or a lie.

We can only sin against the Most High when we put money above God. Finally, sin understands every thought, word, action or omission that saddens God and takes us away from Him. Sin is an obstacle to relationship with God, or the breaking of an already active relationship.

Let us remember that it was the sin of disobedience and rebellion that broke God's relationship with Adam and Eve. Of all the trees in the Garden of Eden, the couple could eat less of the fruit of a given tree. Rebelliousness and a great deal of curiosity led the First Couple to break the close relationship they had with God. The human being is a contestant and a rebel by nature. One of the first words, if not the first, that the child speaks "willingly" is the sonorous "NO", an attitude that the happy parents find wonderful.

If you tell your little son that he should not touch a certain thing, you can write that that is exactly what he will do. Curiosity about the forbidden and the hidden brings to Man a tremendous fascination. Therefore, we understand why many children enter the world of drugs and bad companies, because curiosity exerts very powerful attraction and fascination. The result of this is much suffering. Would it not have been better for children to believe the words of their parents and the holy scriptures?

We can draw a parallel between sin and the criminal act, which can be defined as an anti-social act punishable by the isolation of the offender. Likewise, sin takes us away from God. It is curious that many sins, especially those dealing with human interrelationship in more civilized societies, also constitute a crime. This is not just a coincidence, since legal codifications have received a strong influence from Christianity and Judaism. This happens in relation to false testimony, adultery, murder, theft. Criminal law does not deal with the mere intention of the agent, not yet manifested through an action perceptible by the senses.[2627]

At this point in the reading you might think that none of this has anything to do with you. You consider yourself a good person, who does not commit any crime, who seeks not to harm anyone, who may be a well-placed person in society and who may well occupy church benches. You may consider yourself a righteous person, who does not need to attend church, read the Bible, or commune with God, because you seek not to do actions that harm others.

If so, it is almost certain that you are disregarding two important arguments: 1) sin happens also and mainly in the psychic sphere; 2º) mere indifference to God takes us away from Him. [28]

Unlike what happens in the area of criminal law, the strictly psychic sphere of man is fertile ground for sin: it is where everything begins to happen!

Jesus illustrates this truth by teaching that: "You have heard what has been said: 'You shall not commit adultery. 'But I say to you, anyone who looks at a woman with lust has already committed adultery with her in his heart" (Matthew 5:27 and 28)

Jesus continues: "From within, from the hearts of men, come forth evil intentions: prostitution, robbery, murder, adultery, excessive ambition, malice, malice, fornication, envy, slander, arrogance, folly. All these evil things come out of a man, and they make him unclean." (Mark 7:21-23)

It is not enough to be cleansed of sin on the surface or in appearance only; the Christian must seek purification in the depths of his being, since God hears all our thoughts and knows the heart of each one.[29]

With this in mind, we can better assimilate the biblical passage that says, "there is no righteous man, there is not one, there is no one who understands, there is no one who seeks God. All have gone astray, all together have gone astray; There is no one who does good, there is not one. His throat is an open sepulchre, his tongue utters deceit; The poison of a serpent is under her lips; her mouth is full of cursing and bitterness. His feet are swift to shed blood; There is destruction and disgrace in your ways. They have not known the way of peace, there is no fear of God before their eyes." (Romans 3:10)

The verdict weighs on us that we are all guilty of the practice of sin and need God's mercy. [30]

Jesus was deeply angry with the Pharisees, because they lived by practicing the same sins they forbade the people. They said one thing and they did another. There was a total lack of coherence between what they looked like and what they taught with what they did. At one time, Jesus called them "whitewashed tombs," using the expression we find in Psalm

5:10, to denounce that there was, within these leaders, death and rottenness, and, on the outside, a deceptive appearance of beauty.[31] [32]

Sin makes us unhappy. It grieves us and the Most High and breaks off the relationship between them. God has endowed us with a consciousness of right and wrong, of good and evil. When we sin, our conscience triggers the warning that something is wrong.

Our spirit cries out for fellowship with God. While this is not achieved, we feel greatly empty. It is no wonder that more and more people seek psychological and psychiatric help, forgetting that, often, the cause of their problems is in the spiritual sphere.

The human being without God lives as a slave to sin; He always returns to the practice of it, even if his conscience or spirit does not desire it. It's an ingrained habit. Sin dominates his mind in such a way that he cannot free himself from the sinful tendency.

In this perspective, the apostle Paul speaks of a struggle between the flesh and the spirit:

"13. But how can that be? Didn't the law cause my conviction? How, then, can she be good? No, it was sin, evil as it is, that used what was good to lead me to damnation. So you can see how cunning and deadly and obnoxious he is. For sin uses the good laws of God for its own perverse ends. law, then, is good, and the difficulty is not with it but with me, for I am sold into bondage, with sin as my master. 15. I do not understand myself at all, for I really want to do what is right, but I cannot. I do what I don't want - what I hate. 16. I know perfectly well that what I am doing is wrong, and my bad conscience proves that I agree with these laws that I am breaking. 17. However, I cannot help myself, because I am no longer what I am doing. It is sin within me, which is stronger than I and forces me to do these bad things. 18. I know that I am completely corrupted with regard to my old sinful nature. Whichever way I turn, I can't do good. I want to, but I can't. 19. When I want to do good, I don't do it; And when I try not to miss, I still miss. 20. Now, if I am doing that which I do not want, it is simple to say where the trouble is: sin still holds me in its evil clutches. 21. It seems a fact of life that when I want to do what is right, I inevitably do what is wrong. 22. As for my new nature, I like to do the will of God; 23. yet there is something deep within me, there in my lower nature, that is at war with my mind and wins the fight, making me a slave to the sin that is still within me." (Romans 7:13-23 in version "The Living Bible")14. A

Read this passage in the Jerusalem Bible as well.[33]

Our impulses of human nature are in constant arm wrestling with the spirit. Whoever loves his sinful life loses the opportunity to relate to God. Jesus said, "He that loveth his life loses it, and he that hateth his life in this world shall keep it unto eternal life." (John 12:25)[34]

Even if you try your best to be righteous in your relationship with others, if you do not seek God in your life, you are being indifferent to Him and living in sin.

This statement is related to the meaning we give to our lives. No one better talked about it than Rick Warren. For him, the manufacturer establishes the use of his invention. The consumer needs to read the instruction manual, made by the manufacturer, to understand the use and use of a given good. To understand the purpose of human life, we must turn to the Word of God, which is God's revelation of the subject, that is, our Maker's manual (=Creator). [35]

Revelation has support in the Word of God. The other way to look for the meaning of life is in speculation. People seek the purpose of life outside the Word of God.

For many Americans, the meaning of life lies in achieving the so-called "American dream", that is, enjoying a stable financial life, owning their own home and automobile. Others may say "my life is work", or "my life is my family".

In this form of speculation, people seek meanings within themselves and forget that the Word of God teaches that we were created by and for *God*. As Rick Warren writes, "It is only in God that we discover our origin, our identity, what we mean, our purpose, our importance, and our destiny."[36]

It is important to understand that only the Word of God reveals to us the true purpose. That purpose becomes what God Himself has about us. Human beings are contingent on God and dependent on him: it is he who created us. This means that God is the one who reveals to us His purpose for us.

God's purpose lies in people communing with Him and being saved.

We are in communion with God when we are interested in divine matters. Living with God means being used for His purposes and never using God to achieve our own selfish purposes.

In this panorama, sin is the villain that separates us from God and Jesus urges us to fight it vigorously. Once, Jesus went so far as to recommend that if a part of the body causes us to sin, we must pull it out and throw it into the fire, because it is better to lose one of our members than to have the whole body cast into hell.[37]

In another passage, Jesus warns that we should not fear physical death, nor all that causes this kind of death; but, yes, fear and distance ourselves from everything that causes the death of the soul, referring, also, to sin. Now, if the Christian knows that earthly life constitutes only a passage and that his definitive abode is in the kingdom of heaven, he has the conviction that physical or economic death does not affect him definitively. In the Last Judgment, the spiritual death will be a situation with no return. [38]

When we belong to God's family through Christ, we see life as pilgrims in the world and live in an eternal perspective. [39][40]

In addition to the sinful nature, external influences contribute to the practice of sin. It is no exaggeration to say - like the apostle John - that the world lies in the evil one.[41]

Notwithstanding all the development of civilization and technology, the human being, even in the age of knowledge, has not found happiness within himself and insists on living without God. This produces family and all kinds of disagreements, escapism through the use of drugs and drinks, sexual compulsions, prostitution, infidelities, homicides, thefts, violence, occultism, homosexuality.

A lot of junk has been dumped into our heads through the media, especially the Internet, all *in the name* of supposed freedom. She openly displays a lot of violence and sex. All you have to do is turn on television in prime time and note that there is a lot of apologizing for sin: lying, dishonesty, worldly power, lust and all this is represented by smiling artists, richly dressed and adorned and well-dressed.

It turns out that the media has trivialized and relativized sin. Shows it as if it were something ordinary, normal, with no negative consequences; and often, the sinner ends up getting some benefit from the practice of his reprobate act.

This bombardment of negative images corrupts the mind and affects the consciousness that God has given to each person, making it insensitive. The mind assimilates the projections and judgments that we make of ourselves, of others and of everything that is around us. Children and adolescents are the biggest victims, since they do not have filters to retain only what is good.

Jesus admonishes us to beware of what we hear and see. Jesus teaches that the mouth speaks of what the heart is full of, warning us that we must pay close attention and take care of what we hear and store in our heart. [42]

Jesus teaches that "the lamp of the body is thine eye. If your eye is healthy, your whole body will also be illuminated, but if it is bad, your body will also be dark. So you see that the light in you is not Treva. Therefore, if your whole body is illuminated, without any dark mixture, it will be all illuminated like the lamp, when it illuminates you with your radiance".[43]

In the same order of ideas, the apostle Paul makes the following recommendation: "Finally, brethren, be occupied with all that is true, noble, just, loving, honorable, virtuous, or in any way deserving praise."[44]

The disciples even argued about which of them would be the greatest in the Kingdom of Heaven, having Jesus taught that the greatest in the Kingdom of Heaven will be the one who becomes little as a child (Matthew 18:4). "To be like a child" is not exactly a noble category of Christianity, but a condition for being welcomed by God, as can be drawn from Jesus' words: "Verily I say unto you, Except ye change, and become as little children, ye shall in no wise enter into the kingdom of heaven" (Matthew 18:3)

In this way, Jesus seems to emphasize the natural virtues of children, such as trust in parents, kindness, generosity, solidarity, joy, spontaneity, simplicity, authenticity and detachment, These characteristics are to be sought after and conquered by those who truly seek God.

This subject brings us to the purity of heart and mind that must be associated with Christian practice. The mind is where everything begins, especially sin.

The Biblical book of Proverbs, by Solomon, one of the wisest men who ever lived, teaches us that we must cultivate good company and "flee" from the way of sinners, since for them "wickedness is food and violence is drink" (Chapter 4:14). It is not salutary, nor is it fitting for someone - who seeks God - to sit in the "circle of the scornful" (Psalm 1:1), to disqualify and curse the lives of people who are not there to defend themselves.

It is very important that parents are following the lives of their children and especially the choice they make of their companions, so that they can advise and act before they are influenced by malicious people or those who have a bad education.

Another evil external influence, greatly underestimated, is that exercised by the Evil One and the powers of the air, who want to divert people from truth and life with God.

The fall of Man and his expulsion from the Garden of Eden allowed the Evil One to dominate in some spheres, having been called by Christ the "prince of this world", who has under his command the fallen angels. Devil means accuser, slanderer or slanderer, or Satan, who is the greatest of demons. He was the angel of light who sat next to God, therefore called Lucifer, who led the frustrated rebellion against God in heaven and was expelled from there as the Holy Scriptures teach us: [45] [46] [47]

> "How art thou fallen from heaven, O morning star, son of the morning! How you were cast down, you who weakened the nations. 13. Thou saidst in thine heart, I will ascend into heaven: I will exalt my throne above the stars of God, and I will sit in the mount of the congregation, in the uttermost parts of the north. 14. I will ascend above the highest clouds and be like the Most High. 15. Yet thou shalt be cast out into the kingdom of the dead, into the depths of the deep."

The passage in Ephesians 6:12 reveals a hierarchy of the dark ones headed by Satan. The demonological hierarchy is confirmed by Scripture, when, for example, Christ teaches that a certain kind of demons can only be cast out by prayer and fasting according to Mark 9:29.[4849]

Yet as to the external influences that lead us to sin, we can say that, while God is light, perfect, holy, just and loving, Satan is the darkness and father of lies whose purpose is to destroy the divine creation, whose supreme exponent is the human being. Creation is wonderful and perfect and invites us to wonder. The works of Satan are destructive, although they can often be camouflaged by good things in appearance (the means justifying the ends).

Temptation is one of the devil's principal instruments for the destruction of souls that succumb to it.

The principality of Satan does not find much resistance in the world, because it is enough to invade our psychic sphere in the form of a humanly attractive suggestion, for the Enemy to stimulate us to the practice of sin, or accuse us of a sin committed. We do not sin while we are tempted, but temptation has a terrible power over human weaknesses, which are very well known and exploited by the Devil. There is an unequal struggle for our free will, which lies between the carnal desire often ardent and our spiritual consciousness. Only when we are guarded by the Most High do we receive a supernatural force that enables us to overcome temptation. The Holy Spirit strengthens our free will and helps us to say "no" to temptation.

The Bible reports that the time will come when free will will be practically removed in a totalitarian religious environment where only death awaits those who choose to follow God.[50]

Total freedom and overcoming what humanity has called prejudice are justifications that people have commonly used to pave the way that contradicts God's will, letting themselves be overcome by temptations.

Satan is defined in the Bible as the evil one (Matthew 13:19, 38), prince of demons (Matthew 12:24), prince of the power of the air (Ephesians 2:2), prince of this world (John 14:30), corrupter of the senses (2 Corinthians 11:3), enemy, accuser of the brethren, adversary, roaring lion who seeks someone to devour (1 Peter 5:8), dragon and ancient serpent

(Revelation). The Lord Jesus calls him a murderer, a liar and the father of lies (John 8:44).[51]

Many despise the power of influence of demons, even thinking that they no longer exert influence at the present time, or that their presence is limited to the most disadvantaged and uneducated layers of society.

Demonic power, however, exists and acts with great freedom and without encountering opposition in the world to the point that the evangelist says that the world lies in the evil one.[52]

Satan establishes his lordship in the world and does so with the collaboration of the people, whether they know it or not; whether they follow it openly and consciously or not. About lignos. 1/3 of the illnesses in the world are caused by ma spirits

The Devil and his minions are on the prowl - during the 24 hours of the day - to infiltrate the mind of Man and influence those who consent him to take the path of sin, dressed as angels of light according to 2 Corinthians 11:14. If the Devil revealed his true face, he certainly could not win over so many followers in the present time. [53]

The first great lie of the deceiver leads us to believe that he does not exist. Many people come to the knowledge of God and truth by experiencing the power of darkness, because - from it - one comes to the knowledge of the existence of a spiritual dimension. Knowing it, the Bible becomes seen as a living word; We begin to understand the spiritual battle that will decide the destiny of each one in eternity. In this way, it is likely that people who are freed from demonic oppression and possession will become active Christians by virtue of the spiritual truth which they have assimilated by their own experience.

Thus, Satan did not choose as the main strategy for today, to show his true face of destruction and hatred. This is the greatest diabolical lie of the present and the Devil's interest is that people do not experience the spiritual dimension, because it will bring them to the knowledge of God, the devil and the fact that we are the target of a spiritual battle.

Who cannot see this scenario, probably will have a selfish and immediate perspective of life, seeking the maximum of earthly pleasure. The Evil One is very pleased with the alienation that this deception causes in people and even in part of Christendom.

While the evil one does not find much resistance in the world, he reserves for believers a greater dedication. Believers are tempted more openly, so that they cannot discern between freedom and debauchery, prosperity and love of money, eroticism and lust/lust, cunning and dishonesty, meaningless spiritual and ritual worship, Christian dynamism and author-seekingrecognition or social projection.

Perhaps the name that best defines Satan is "the father of lies". Satan does and will do everything to try to achieve his goals of destruction, even through what he most hates: the practice of good. But this "good" is produced only in appearance, which will cause many to be entangled in their lying plots as Jesus warned. [54]

The devil's stratagem comprises the use of half-truths to cover up his higher purpose. Let us remember the cunning argument of the devil in the garden of Eden:

> "The serpent was the most cunning of all the beasts of the fields that Iahweh God had made. And she said unto the woman, Said God, Cannot ye eat of all the trees of the garden? ' woman answered to the serpent: We may eat of the fruit of the trees of the garden. 3. But of the fruit of the tree which is in the midst of the garden. God said, You shall not eat of him, you shall not touch him on pain of death. ' serpent then said to the woman, Nay, you shall not die! 5. But God knoweth that in the day that ye eat thereof your eyes shall be opened, and ye shall be as gods, versed in good and evil." ' 2. A4. A

First, the devil managed to establish a strong doubt in Eve's mind, remembering that God allowed her to eat the fruit of all the trees in the garden. Shrewdly, Satan recalls the general rule (what could be done), making the exception (what should not be done) apparently understood in the general rule.

Then the devil used two half-truths, which worked as a deceptive stimulus (temptation), to say that this fruit would transform them into gods, versed in good and evil, and that their eyes would open.

In fact, the eyes of the First Couple were opened, because they were aware of their fall (loss of holiness) and their departure from God (loss of communion).

Satan's main goal, however, was for the First Couple to have his death decreed, and he succeeded. Satan knew that God would watch over the fulfillment of his Word and that the sanction (death) would be applied in case of disobedience. [55]

The First Couple who had been created to live eternally, with the fall, came to have a temporally limited life. The Bible does not report the spiritual destiny of the First Couple after their physical death.

Satan's greater purpose is to drive people away from God and, therefore, to contribute to their spiritual demise.

How does the devil act these days? Just as he acted in the garden of Eden, with subterfuges, with half-truths, with deceptive stimuli, all always covering up the truth he wants to attack. He also acts by casting oppression, dominating people who are imprisoned by a specific sin, such as lust and lust, as well as by causing illness.

The truth that Satan attacks is salvation; He seeks people's death and perdition. On the other hand, Jesus is the good shepherd:

> "11. I am the good shepherd: the good shepherd lays down his life for his sheep. 12. The hireling, who is not a true shepherd and to whom the sheep do not belong, when he sees the wolf coming, abandons the sheep and flees; And the wolf taketh them, and scattereth them. 13. For he is a hired hand, and of little importance to his sheep. 14. I am the good shepherd, I know my sheep, and my sheep know me, 15 as my Father knows me, and I know the Father, and I lay down my life for the sheep." (John, chapter 10, Bible version, ecumenical translation.)

Satan continues to use God's Word to deceive even the elect. He whispers in people's ears, "Didn't Christ call them to freedom?" Or, "If sins can be forgiven, there is no harm in committing them." [56][57]

The theme of freedom will be developed in more detail in the topic "sanctifying oneself", but let us consider, for the time being, the statement that Jesus frees us from the bondage of sin. This produces true deliverance, because we feel enough and spiritually strong that we no longer have the inclination to sin and can say "no" to sin that our spirit wants to reject by exercising a genuine free will. We no longer live immersed in sin. Sin ceases to be a guest in our heart to be an accident of course.

Satan wants to establish the lie that certain sins can be committed in the name of God's supposed infinite tolerance.

Nobody better be fooled about that. Regrettably, it has already been established that deception that lust and sexual relations outside of marriage are not sins, or that they are sins tolerated by God.

It takes care of an untruth that leads to perdition! We cannot expect to be saved if we live immersed in sin, or if we practice it deliberately, especially after we know the truth.

The apostle Paul writes:

> "What shall we say then? Will we continue to sin so that grace may increase? Not at all! We who die to sin, how can we continue to live in it? Or do you not know that all of us who were baptized, were baptized at his death? (Romans 6:1-3, version of the NIV Study Bible). em Cristo Jesus

> For if we sin willingly and with the knowledge of the truth, there are no more sacrifices for sins. Only a tremendous judgment awaits us and the ardour of a fire that will consume the

adversaries. Whoever transgresses the Law of Moses is condemned to death, without mercy, on the basis of two or three witnesses. Can you then imagine what even harsher punishment he will deserve who trampled the Son of God at his feet, and profaned the blood of the covenant in which he was sanctified, and blessed the Spirit of grace? We know, in fact, who says: Revenge belongs to me, I will repay! And again, The Lord shall judge his people. How terrible it is to fall into the hands of the living God!" (Hebrews 9:26-30)

Worldly life and Christian life are not reconciled, just as water and oil are not mixed. You can't have heaven on earth!

The end of the times will be marked by the increase of the diabolical performance, because the time of the Enemy is running out. Your weapon will continue to be your trademark: the lie, yet refined, but always true-looking. So much so that the number of the beast, which is 666, can be explained by the proximity of its elements to the number 7, which means the number of perfection and eternity.

7 has a special meaning for God: 7 thus corresponds to the cycle of creation, God having rested and sanctified the seventh day; seven are the turns that God commanded the Hebrews to go around Jericho (Joshua 6:4); 7 times 70 are the

times that Jesus commanded us to forgive (Matthew 18:21). This is not counting the times the number 7 appears in the book of Revelation (7 angels, 7 spirits, 7 stars, etc.).

The number 666, therefore, may well indicate the appearance of perfection and normality, while in fact the Christian religious institutions and even the church of Christ will be, little by little, suffocated by the Father of Lies, who will attack the foundations of Christianity, using ostensibly the name of Jesus Christ, but in the shadows calling on demons even to perform cures. [58] [59]

The Church of Christ will be attacked in its rudiments, mainly in the capacity of sharing (speaking of Jesus) and personal edification (communicating with Jesus).

Churches will continue to exist, but leaders will be deceivers. Satan will establish a system of government in which people will fail to pronounce the precious name of Jesus Christ; The songs in the churches will no longer mention the name of Jesus, because in this way the Evil One will be directly attacking salvation, since the Bible teaches that there is no other Name below heaven by which we must be saved.

Acting more aggressively, the Devil causes sickness, oppression, and possessions in people.

The devil also uses occultism, creature worship, magic, and other practices that are nothing more than veneration of Satan and an instrument of invocation of evil powers. All this, however, constitutes an abomination to God and deceives those who seek divinity through these practices.

Demons use various tricks and dress themselves as angels of light to be seen, in the eyes of the unwary, as good spirits, hiding their real purpose of diverting people from the true doctrine.[60]

One should not attribute to demons, however, every order of illnesses, unemployment, illnesses and negative events of life. If something goes wrong, immediately suggest some a "download" session to remove the "backrests" and "moorings". Many of these occurrences are explained by natural or conjunctural reasons, and most of the time, the Evil One acts in the lives of those who consent, even unconsciously.

In this regard, says the apostle John: "We know that whosoever is born of God sinneth not; God-begotten keeps him and the Evil One cannot touch him." As we have seen above, if the believer is reached, he can receive deliverance. Where there is light, there can be no darkness and vice versa. [61]

The Bible prophesies that the antichrist will have political and economic dominion, so that the battle will leave the strictly spiritual and mental ground to transform itself into a time of intense and great tribulation, marked by the open persecution of true Christians who persevere to the end. [62]

Jesus calls the outcome of human history an "abomination of desolation" and explains that "in those days there will be such tribulation as has not been since the beginning of the world that God has created until now, and never will be. And if the Lord had not shortened these days, there would be no life saved: But because of the elect whom he chose, he shortened the days". [63]

We can trust that, even in these terrible days, Jesus will never leave believers orphaned and his promises will be as valid in the future as they are today and were in the past. The Holy Scriptures assure us that your reign will be eternal. [64]

2   *Origin of sin and intellectual autonomy*

Without intending to exhaust the approach of the so-called cousin *caused sin*[65], who participates in works far more detailed and superior to it, it is enough to consider that the first cause of [66][67][68][69][70]sin is not associated with the act of creation, because sin is linked to the destruction and destitution of reality (= creation) according to Berkouwer, given that the Bible and the life of Jesus reveal to us that God is love, light, holy and just, this being a fundamental biblical knowledge (aprioristic)which supports the development of other truths.

Because man is created in the image and likeness of God, it is difficult to accept that the origin of evil and sin is evident and natural, in what we support Berkouwer.[71]

So much so that God, in contemplating his creation, saw that everything was "very good", not only the spirit of man generated by the divine breath, but the modeled body of the clay of the soil. And when God saw that man was alone, he created woman to be one flesh. And all this was very good! [72][73][74][75]

Considering the perfection of the creative act, where did sin come from? Perhaps a convincing and seemingly paradoxical answer can be found in the fact that man was created with intellectual autonomy, in the image and likeness of God.

Both angels and men were created with free will and intellectual autonomy, so that Adam and Lucifer rebelled against God.

The First Man was also created to administer his life and the Garden of Eden with almost total autonomy and freedom, being able to make his own decisions by carrying out his daily tasks, receiving the company of God at the end of each day's afternoon.

This intellectual autonomy aroused, in the first man, the foolish feelings that would lead him to detach himself from God, despising the severe warning that disobedience would lead him to death.

The adjective "foolish" clearly describes the acts of the First Couple who lived in a perfect world within an eternal expectation. Perhaps the explanation for this lies in pride, in the expectation of gaining knowledge at the divine level, or in unchallenged and senseless curiosity.[76]

Original sin has caused so much perplexity that Berkouwer, although he believes that the cause of sin lies in man, considers it enigmatic and admits an external cause to explain the "transition from the original goodness of creation to the meaningless vanity" of man. [77]

Anyway, there was a certain space for the decision-making of the First Couple, which we can call free will.

We may wonder why God put the tree of the knowledge of good and evil before the First Couple. The most accepted explanation is that God desired to test man's faithfulness and wished him to fulfill his precepts spontaneously.

According to the opinion of Watchmann Nee, God would have placed before Adam and Eve the two trees: that of Life and that of the knowledge of good and evil, so that they could make use of the prerogative of choice ("free will"). The tree of Life, according to that Writer, "is God himself, because God is life, the highest expression of life, as well as the source and aim of life... If Adam took the tree of life, he would participate in the life of God and thus become a "son" of God, in the sense of having in himself a life derived from God. We would then have the life of God in union with man: a race of men having in themselves the life of God and living in constant [78][79]*dependence on God for the manifestation of that life.* If, on the other hand, Adam turned in the opposite direction and took the fruit of the tree of the knowledge of good and evil, he would then develop his own humanity naturally and separately from God. Achieving a high degree of feats and knowledge by his achievements and acquisitions as being self-sufficient, would have in himself the power to form opinions independently of God; *but he would not have the divine life in himself.* That was therefore the alternative before him. Choosing the way of the Spirit, independent and autonomous, judging and acting separately from God. The history of humanity is the result of the choice Adam made". path of obedience, could become a "child" of God, depending on God for the manifestation of his life or, following the natural course, he could, so to speak, give the final touch on himself, becoming a being

The Most High put to the test the faithfulness of the First Couple, strictly forbidding him to eat of the forbidden fruit, harshly warning him that disobedience would lead him to death.

It is not rare that the Most High should have tested the obedience of Man, so it was, for example, with Abraham, who was commanded to sacrifice his son; with Job, whose faithfulness to God was tested against the loss of his heritage, his family, his friends, and finally his health; the Jewish people were put to the test for God to verify whether or not he "will walk in my law". [80][81]

God tested the Jewish people for 40 years in the desert by making them walk in circles many times, because the people were stiff-necked.

Returning to the First Couple, consider the reader that by that time the angels led by Lucifer had already been expelled from the heavenly abode by virtue of the rupture of fidelity. The Lord God had already experienced rebellion on the part of the one who was one of His most important creatures (Lucifer) and it is possible that the tree of the knowledge of good and evil was a way to prove the faithfulness of the First Couple.

Even in the face of the severe warnings of the Most High, the First Couple made use of their ability to make choices, taking and eating of the forbidden fruit, and thereupon ceased to be innocent and had spiritual death.

Man's free will means that he can act freely, but not that he is a being absolutely free and independent of God, so much so that he will be judged as a consequence of that same free will and morally responsible for the choices he makes.

The Word of God, in the book of Sirach (Ecclesiastes), teaches us that the Most High **"gave** no man [82]**permission to sin", gathering that he delivered** man, as a result of his sins, "to his own will[83]".

In fact, the Most High abhors sin and could not condone its practice, but decided to abandon Man to his "inclination" and did so moved by the addition of his mercy, so that it would not exterminate him completely. [84]

Consider, also, that the Most High has never given up the right to judge his creature and certainly will do so even in the future, so that he can never be the arbiter of himself as to the destiny of what is more dear to him: his spiritual guidance. [85]

Probably our first reaction is to blame Adam and Eve for drawing death to humanity. However, when we think so, we forget that humanity proves to be unwise. Certainly, we're no better than Adam and Eve.

We must reflect on the barbarism that humanity would be if it were not for the spread of Christian principles, which have changed the face of the earth. Even today, with all the progress in the areas of knowledge, the human being does not find balance in himself.

It is important to stress that Christianity is not a philosophical current, but the true and only path for sharing God's presence through a daily relationship.

The same crisis of folly that led the First Couple to disobey God is what leads man, today, to take refuge in drink, to commit marital infidelity, to say improprieties to his neighbor in a moment of exaltation, to consider himself self-sufficient and independent of God.

Was intellectual autonomy a "bad" thing created by God? No, not at all. But what was very good was misrepresented by the man himself and the evil one. Man misused the thinking ability that God gave him for his happiness, making it an instrument for his own destruction.

We are undoubtedly responsible for our actions and if we choose sin it is certain that we will be condemned. But it is in our hands to make the best choice: choose, therefore, life with Jesus!

3   *The commandments of God*

In the previous chapter, we sought to present the reasons for living in communion with God and the corrupting minds that draw us away from God, as well as the consequences of that departure. Now is the time to speak in more detail about the behaviors that violate God's commandments and that are sins.

Rather, however, we will make a quick foray into the history of Abraham, because God established with him the great first covenant, to then situate this first covenant in relation to the second, and both in relation to sin.

Sarai, Abram's wife, bore him no children. She asked Abram to take as wife his Egyptian servant, named Hagar, so that she might conceive a child of his. Thus it was done, and Hagar became pregnant. Sarai, jealous, mistreated Hagar, causing the flight of Hagar and the son she had had with Abram, called Ishmael. The angel of God found Hagar in the wilderness, near the fountain on the way to Shur, and told her to return to her mistress, because the child she was expecting

- whom she should call Ishmael - would have countless posterity.

God's promise was fulfilled, since Ishmael became the father of the Arab peoples. And the angel said unto him, That his son shall be "a foal of man, and his hand against all, and the hand of all against him: He will settle down before all his brethren". [86]

God wanted to make another great covenant with Abram, who became called Abraham, because it would make him extremely fruitful and father of many nations and would give the land of Canaan, in an everlasting possession, to the people born of the seed of Abraham, who would be his people. It is the covenant maintained with the Hebrew people, sealed with circumcision. [87] [88]

God spoke to Abraham: [89]

> "Your wife Sarai will no longer be called Sarai, but her name is Sarah. I will bless her and give her a son; And I will bless her, and she shall become nations, and out of her shall come kings of peoples. Abraham fell on his face and laughed, for he said to himself: Shall a child of a man a hundred years old be born, and Sarah who is ninety years old shall give birth? ' Abraham said to God, Oh! May Ishmael live

> before you! ' But God said, No, but your wife
> Sarah will give you a son: you shall call him
> Isaac; I will establish my covenant with him, as
> an everlasting covenant, to be his God and that
> of his race after him. For Ishmael also, I have
> heard thee, I bless him, I will make him fruitful,
> I will cause him to grow exceedingly; He shall
> beget twelve princes, and I will make him a
> great nation. But my covenant I will establish
> with Isaac, which Sarah will give birth to next
> year, at this station"".

God's promises have been and are being fulfilled. The sons of Abraham: Isaac and Ishmael, respectively, are the father of the Jews and the Arabs. Ishmael had twelve sons who became clan chiefs as reported in the book of Genesis chapter 25, verse 16. [90]

At the UN he recommended the creation in Palestine of two new states, a Jew and an Arab, as well as the creation of a neutral and internationalized zone around Jerusalem. This provoked armed conflicts between Jews, Arabs and Englishmen. Although the Jews were outnumbered, they captured the port of Java, causing the escape of about 700,000 Arabs. On 14 May the new state of Israel was proclaimed.

There, the ancient land of Canaan, came Jews from all over the world. 1947, a

The first great covenant of God, established with the Jews, was sealed with the circumcision of all men from among the household and servants of Abraham.

Isaac begat Jacob and Jacob begat twelve sons who gave birth to the twelve tribes of Israel, the name Jacob received when he engaged in a fight with the angel of God. One of Jacob's sons, named Joseph, became high authority in Egypt, facilitating the move of the Jews to Egypt. After Joseph's death, the Jews were enslaved in Egypt for 400 years, until God mightily brought them out of that land through Moses.[91]

On Mount Sinai, God granted to the Jews, led by Moses, the ten commandments, namely:

> "Thou shalt have no other gods before me.
>
> Thou shalt not make thee any graven image, or any likeness of any thing that is above, in the heavens, or under, or on the earth, or in the waters under the earth.
>
> He will not bow down to these gods, and you shall not serve them: for I, Yahweh, your God, am a jealous God, avenging the iniquity of the

fathers in the children unto the third and fourth generation of them that hate me; And I show mercy unto a thousand generations to them that love me and keep my commandments.

You shall not take the name of Iahweh, your God, in vain, because Iahweh will not let him who takes his name in vain go unpunished.

Remember Saturday to sanctify him. You shall work six days, and do all your works. But the seventh day is the Sabbath of Iahweh thy God. You shall do no work, neither you, nor your son, nor your daughter, nor your beast, nor the stranger that is in your gates. For in six days Yahweh made heaven, and earth, and sea, and all that they contain, but rested on the seventh day: So Iahweh blessed the Sabbath day and sanctified it.

Honour thy father and thy mother, that thy days may be long in the land which Iahweh thy God giveth thee.

You will not kill.

Thou shalt not commit adultery.

You will not steal.

You shall not bear false witness against your neighbor.

Thou shalt not desire thy neighbour's house; thou shalt not desire his wife, nor his

<blockquote>manservant, nor his maidservant, nor his ox, nor his donkey, nor any thing that pertaineth to thy neighbour."</blockquote>

Such is the importance given by God to worship, that He dedicated the first three commandments to it. Worship consists in worshipping God, fearing Him and reverencing Him as the Superior, Creator, Sovereign, and Almighty Being.

Only before God should we bow, worship, and worship. One should never participate in cults to deities, pagan gods, mythological or unknown gods on the false assumption that there is any kind of association with the Almighty God.

Idolatry is the total rupture with God. Let us remember that the Lord God foretold Moses, shortly before his death, that the Israelites broke the covenant by virtue of the prostitution of the people with the gods of the foreigners. [92]

The Word of God is very enlightening and thorough in regard to idolatry. Thus, we can be sure that no image, symbol or artifact can represent the True God, considering that He does not allow us to reduce Him to such a representation.

God also made known to us his name, which is YHWH, which is pronounced Iahvé or Iahô[93], *which means "I AM THAT*

I WILL BE". It is the name by which God called himself on Mount Sinai, when Moses asked the Lord what he would say to the Hebrews if they asked him who had sent him. [94]

For Father Aleksandr Mien, the name of God means "one who possesses the essence because it exists before the whole sensible world". According to this same scholar, "from the fourth century, out of respect for the name of God, it was forbidden (exceptions apart) to pronounce the word Iahweh. To designate the name of God, the noun [95]*Adonai* the Lord was used in the oral discourse. The written texts, reminding the reader of the prohibition, noted the vowels of the word Adonai under the letters of the name of JHWH. From this derives the altered name of 'Jehovah' which was in use in the Bible for a time".

GOD ALSO IS ALMIGHTY (Genesis 16:1; Exodus 6:3), in Hebrew "El Shadai"; THE LORD OF HOSTS.[96]

Also the Bible in the Ecumenical Translation reports that the custom of not pronouncing the name of God from the fourth century on made it difficult to know for certain with which vowels the name of God was pronounced.[97]

In an attempt to garner sympathizers among the Athenians, the apostle Paul emphasized their "almost religiosity" by making the inscription "to the unknown god" on their altars. Paul cleverly criticized their practices: [98]

> "The God who created the universe and all that is in it, he who is the Lord of heaven and earth, does not dwell in times built by the hand of men and his service does not require human hands, as if he lacked anything, because he gives everyone life and breath and everything...
>
> Therefore, since we are of the race of God, we should not think that the divinity resembles gold, silver, or marble, sculpture of art and man's imagination. And, behold, God, disregarding these times of ignorance, announces to men now that all, and everywhere, must be converted. For he has set a day in which he must judge the world justly by the man whom he has appointed, according to the assurance which he has given to all, by raising him from the dead."

In this way, only IHWH, the one God and Almighty, should render praise and worship.

God has made us sufficiently aware of Him in the Holy Scriptures, especially the only correct way to worship Him. Thus, the believer should never worship symbols, deities, unknown beings, statues, images, or any other personification than our God (sufficiently) known in the Bible.

Take, for example, verse 19 of the first chapter of Romans, when the Apostle Paul, speaking to Gentiles, stated, "For what may be known of God is manifest to them: God has made it known to them." (BTE)

Jesus Christ occupies the position of God's only begotten Son and is not confused with the one God (Yahweh). Likewise, the Holy Spirit is a Person distinct from the Father and the Son. I coined the expression "Heavenly Counsel" to address these Three Persons. The confrontation of this theme, by its complexity, escapes the limits of this work and will be object ("The love (in)conditional of God"). dissertation in my next book

Our god can be money, when we live in its service and in its function, considering material goods as the most important, and not just an instrument of enjoyment of a dignified life. Christ had already warned:

> "No one can serve two masters. For either he will hate the one, and love the other, or he will hold fast to the first, and despise the second. You cannot serve God and money."[99]

In the book of Timothy, Chapter 6, we find the following message:

> "7. For we have brought nothing into the world, neither can we take anything from it. 8 If therefore we have food and clothing, let us prove ourselves by it. 9. Now they that desire to be rich fall into temptation and a snare, and into many foolish and pernicious desires, which plunge men into ruin and perdition. 10. For the root of all evil is the love of money, wherewith some have turned away from the faith, and afflict themselves with manifold torments."

When we cling to God for the sole purpose of prosperity, we are trying to make a bargain with God.

Many important biblical characters, who were men of God, were prosperous, such as Abraham and Joseph (son of Jacob) and it is common to find in the Old Testament promises of prosperity to the Jews, but with the warning that they should practice the Word:

> "Ye shall keep the words of this covenant, and put them into effect, that ye may prosper in all that ye do." (Deuteronomy 29:8, BTE)

The recommendation contained in Psalm 62:10, however, sounds timely and timely:

"If your fortune increases, do not fix your heart on it." (BTE)

We must not forget that Jesus promised the following: the believer will receive from God food and clothing, as well as the promise to the children that when they first seek the kingdom of God, "all this will be given to you in addition" (Bte, Matthew 6:33), referring to Jesus' needs as food, drink, and clothing. [100]

If I accept my sonship with God, I now have all the prerogatives of a son. Probably, in that condition, I will work harder than my Father's servants and servants, because I have an interest in defending his cause which, by extension, also belongs to me. The child does not work for the father by a bond of obligation or servility; the Father conquers through love all the confidence of the son and he works hard and quiet because he knows that all his needs will be supplied.

Thus, when we accept the sonship that God offers us through Jesus, we leave our condition as creatures and become his children, And we get all the spiritual blessings that the Father wants to give us, and we also receive all the material goods that we need, both for our personal needs and for whatever is necessary for the Father's cause.

Both blessings and prosperity are only granted by the Father in the same order of promise (Matthew 6:33): first the cause of God and then the addition of all things.

Another situation is wealth. How much property does a person have to be considered rich? We're talking about considerable assets. Of course, if this collection is used in the service of God, there will be no love for money.

God can interfere supernaturally so that a person has prosperity, not to mention, of course, that God has given him the ability and intelligence to obtain a patrimony.

In many cases, however, the Father puts us in the situation of receiving only what is necessary and, as children, we will be honored and happy because we have enough for life and nothing will certainly fail us.

Prosperity also depends, in our days, on political, economic and personal conditions, but the transformation through which a child of God passes, in his spirit, in his character, and in his temperament, they encourage him to seek and obtain better living conditions, and the Father rejoices in the Son and knows that he will manage his financial life well to honor and dignify the Father's cause.

Faith in Jesus, in many parts of the world, is a reason for persecutions and killings (Muslim-majority countries, e.g.), repeating the records of Christian history, and it is certain that the end times will be marked by death in its most comprehensive meaning.

Jesus denounced the love of riches, stating that hardly a rich man will enter the Kingdom of God, and this is probably due to the tendency to serve money and live for himself by accommodating himself. According to Jesus, he already has his consolation.[101][102]

Jesus passed on to the disciples the altruism in community life, so much so that the early Church required the new believers to deliver, at the apostles' feet, all their possessions, which were divided among the believers as needed.[103]

This model lost strength due to the probable impoverishment of the early Jewish Christians, who perhaps sold the goods that provided them means of survival, remembering that the Christians of Judea were helped by the brothers of Antioch on the occasion of great famine (Acts 11:28-30).

Concerning the divine providence of our needs, the Word dictates a priority order: first, we must seek the Kingdom of God and its righteousness, and all the material things we need will be added to us.[104]

If the motivation to seek God is only prosperity, a person who has this goal in view will certainly totally lose the little faith he possesses as well as the few savings he has garnered from performing the "sacrifice" that some religious denominations have been advocating to increase their heritage. The question, however, is the spiritual cost, the theological consistency and the foundation for this thesis, considering that the ends should not justify the spiritual means and results, in this case they will certainly appear ephemeral.

We must contribute financially to the ministries of God, but as gratitude for what we have already received from Him, and not to bargain for future blessings.

Many worship the clairvoyance and, with this, worship the entities they invoke. The invocation of dead people or spirits constitutes an abomination to God, who proclaims: [105]

> "in thy midst there is not found any... that maketh omen, or oracle, or divination, or that practiseth enchantments, or that searcheth spirits, or diviners, or calleth the dead; For he that doeth these things is an abomination unto the Iahweh" (Deuteronomy 18:10-12);
>
> "You shall not turn to the necromancers, nor consult the diviners, for they would defile you" (Leviticus 19:31);
>
> "Whosoever shall use the necromancers and diviners to commit fornication with them, I will turn against that man, and cut him off from among his people" (Leviticus 20:6); "the man or woman who is a necromancer or soothsayer among you shall be put to death; they shall be stoned, and their blood shall fall upon them" (Leviticus 20:27)

God, who is jealous, does not approve of man making images of animals, demons, deities created by human hands, or people and considering them as his god, given that Yahweh is the only God.

God has a great appreciation for worship, not only because He has dealt with the subject in three commandments, but because it is one of the few ordinances accompanied by a blessing; and what a blessing! It consists of the following: God will have mercy not only on the one who keeps the commandment, but on the one who is the posterity of the commandment, reaching up to a thousand generations!

We can understand the reason for the importance of the commandment by the fact that worship concerns the direct relationship between God and man and constitutes the way in which it directly externalizes love to God.

The first three commandments forbid idolatry. God does not want us to have other gods before Him, nor does He want us to worship an image as if it represented the Living God. God is Spirit and His worshippers must worship Him in spirit and in truth as Jesus teaches. [106]

The Apostle John, the Beloved of the Master Jesus, exclaims that "no one has ever seen God: the only begotten Son, who is turned to the bosom of the Father, the Father has made him known". It is God Himself who warns, "You cannot see My face, for man cannot see Me and continue to live." (Exodus 33:20) [107]

If we do not see God, how can we form an image of him? Even if we had seen Him, He would not allow us to make an image of Him. The great honor of seeing God and watching with Him is reserved for a few, such as the angels of children and the saved who are pure in heart. [108] [109]

On Mount Sinai, God appeared in the form of a burning bush. Moses asked God what he should call Him in case the Jews ask him who sent him. To this God said, "I AM has sent me to you... Yahweh, the God of your fathers, the God of Abraham, the God of Isaac, and the God of Jacob, has sent me to you." [110]

To reduce God to an image is to belittle him, to cease to fear him, to respect him, and to honor him. Let us remember that Jacob also asked God what He was called, to which God answered with another question: "Why ask you my name?"[111]

God is, quite simply. We cannot limit it or reduce it to an image. Undoubtedly, God acts with love and mercy and is slow to anger, but it can also be terrible as described in the book of Hebrews 10:29-31: "Whoever transgresses the law of Moses is condemned to death without mercy on the basis of two or three witnesses. Can you then imagine what even harsher punishment he will deserve who trampled the Son of God at his feet, and profaned the blood of the covenant in which he was sanctified, and blessed the Spirit of Grace? We know, in fact, who says: Revenge belongs to me, I will repay! And again, The Lord shall judge his people. How terrible it is to fall into the hands of the Living God!"

Holy men may be revered, as men of flesh and blood who are, but never worshipped. Even the saints who were raised to eternity were not invested in the function of God's intercessors. John the Baptist, for example, was recognized by Jesus as the most important man born of woman, having not worshipped or recognized as an intercessor between God and men. however, any biblical basis for it to be [112]

Thus, it is unbiblical to worship human persons, or to regard them as intercessors before God. Every Christian - who feels in his heart the desire to separate for the service of God - becomes sanctified independently of any process of human recognition. Therefore, the saints are Christian persons who have or have had a consecrated life in the service of God.

Christians must intercede for one another in prayer, but always addressing their prayers exclusively to God, with no support in God's Word for intercessory prayer for saints.

In Brazil, the cult of image is very strong, and the most humble people often worship the sculptures as if they were their gods, or intercessors of God. This constitutes a repulsive action for God.

It is contrary to the Word of God to ask intercession for dead people, since the only intercessor between us and God is the savior Jesus Christ, who overcame death by being resurrected.

In the present century, the cult of Mary is being spread and stimulated by some religious institutions. For this religious segment, according to the article "The feminine face of God", published in Galileo magazine number 149, Mary was not only a reference of life, or a person whose life was consecrated to the service of God, she was the feminine face of God, the fourth divine person together with God the Father, God the Son, and God the Holy Spirit.

Pope John Paul II referred to Mary as "co-counselor" on several occasions, and this qualification could be the fifth dogma to be proclaimed by the Catholic Church concerning Mary, who is already considered "mother of God" (first dogma), "perpetual virgin" (second dogma), "immaculate conception" (third dogma), and "assumption" (fourth dogma).

While it is true that Mary had a prominent role in her role of receiving Jesus who was formed from the Divine Holy Spirit, there is nothing in the biblical accounts that gives her special importance, whether in the years of Jesus' apostolate or in early church times. On the contrary, the Bible reports that Mary was always a preserved person among Christians.

At one point, when Jesus was speaking to the people, he was interrupted by someone who informed him that his mother and brothers were outside, looking for him, to which He replied, "Who is my mother and who are my brothers? And he stretched out his hand unto his disciples, and said, Behold my mother and my brethren. For whosoever shall do the will of my heavenly Father, the same is my brother, and my sister, and my mother" (Matthew 12:48 to 50) The Bible records, therefore, that Mary was not in a higher degree of importance than any other disciple, or follower, who did the will of the Father. [113]

Note that Jesus did not include himself as "born of woman" by referring to John the Baptist, his contemporary, as the greatest among those born in this way. With these words, Jesus also emphasizes that his earthly birth was a supernatural phenomenon, not considering himself to be "born of a woman", because, if he had done so, he would have put his Name before that of John the Baptist, whereas he was not worthy to untie the Master's sandals, Jesus having an infinitely greater testimony than that of John the Baptist, who only prepared the way of God the Son.[114]

Mary will always be considered blessed among men for having consented to the Lord God to biologically form her Son in her womb, but there is no biblical foundation for her to be considered as an "intercessor" between the faithful and God, where the admission of this premise would be the same as nullifying the plan of salvation, rendering void both the death and the resurrection of the one High Priest, who is Christ.

The Bible reveals that:

> "Jesus is the stone rejected by you, the builders, which has become the cornerstone. And **there is no salvation in any other;** For there is no salvation under heaven in any other: For there is **no** other name under heaven given among men by which we must be saved." (Acts 4:11-12)

Another beautiful biblical passage that speaks of the theme is found in Philippians:

> "Be of the same mind as there was also in you, for he, standing in the form of God, judged not to be equal with God as usurpation; but emptied himself, taking the form of a servant, becoming the likeness of men; and, recognized in human form, humbled himself, becoming obedient unto death, and death on the cross. Wherefore God also hath highly exalted him, and given him the name that is above every name, that at the name of Jesus every knee should bow, in heaven, on earth, and under the earth, and every tongue should confess that Jesus Christ is Lord, unto the glory of God the Father. (Chapter 3:5-11)em Cristo Jesus

Thus, we must revere the memory of Mary for being graced with the privilege of receiving, in her womb, the incarnation of God the Son, but never expect intermediation of her part between us and God, since there is only one Advocate and High Priest who performs this function, which coincides with the person of Jesus Christ. There is no antechamber for salvation, represented by Mary, which would stand between Jesus and believers.

Satanism or occultism, in its essence, is the worship of the Devil himself and the evil entities. Curious is the report published in the "Journal of Religions", third edition, November 2003, page 28:

> "It is not known how many they are, where they are concentrated, or what their rituals are. But according to historian Carlos Nogueira of USP, satanic movements emerged around the 18th century, when the idea of the Devil as a friend of man gains strength: Satan becomes a symbol of joy and freedom. Often confused with occultists and practitioners of magic, Satanists are, in general, young, upper-class people thirsting for fame and power. The 31-year-old *designer* Flávio de Carvalho was a member of a satanic sect of Californian origin in the 1980s. After almost committing suicide in a moment of despair, when he was still a devil worshipper, the designer turned his *life* around 13 years ago. Now, he believes in Jesus and in God, responsible for his deliverance, according to him, despite not strictly following any religion. Check your testimonial to the MAGAZINE OF RELIGIONS:

I wanted to know the mysteries. I sold my soul for it and got paid. To Satanists, you are your own god, you do what you want. Today Satanism preaches the "I" above all, so vanity is the favorite sin. But it's a trap, a dazzling business. You get there badly from your legs and they fix it. For about three years, you've lived everything you ever dreamed of. Then they demand obedience and the charge is very serious.

You don't join a cult on the Internet. You're invited, they find you. Their method of grooming is to target parties, *college* campuses, and bookstores, where people with a good level of knowledge are. I made a blood pact to be accepted. For young people, the advantages are having money, sex with beautiful people, success and fame. Getting in is easy, but getting out is hard. Nobody can get out on their own.

Halloween parties aren't harmless. There is a whole ritual, in the type of music, of food, of drink. There is also the feast of the Passover, in which a person is sacrificed to commemorate the death of Jesus.

I began to disobey some things, to doubt the prince of the universe, who is Satan, and I suffered retaliation. I saw that his love for me was not so great. '"

Satanism is growing all over the world, gaining more and more adherents, who are attracted by the material rewards and sense of power that are apparently bestowed on their faithful.

Satanism employs the Bible so that its adherents do the opposite of what is taught there.

Not infrequently, we follow on television news the trial of cult leaders who sacrificed children and excised their organs in satanic rituals.

Satan is nicknamed the prince of this world, but Jesus is greater than he. As it is written, "Little children, you belong to God, and have overcome false prophets, because the greater is he who is in you, and he who is in the world." He who is of God is invested with all power to prevent, through prayer, the onslaughts of the Adversary which are manifested as oppressions, possessions, and evil suggestions.[115]

Believers are not free from evil attacks, indeed, they are the preferred targets of the Adversaries.

The fourth commandment concerns the name of God. We must not pronounce God's name in vain. God allows us to elevate our thoughts and words to him and we should not distort this communication. We must remember that God made us in his image and likeness: just as the power of God is manifested by the word, so also he manifests himself among believers by the word spoken or mentalized by them. To speak the name of God in vain is to despise our Lord. Thus, it is completely wrong to mention God's name as if it were any form of interjection. There are people who use the name of God in totally unreasonable situations, such as when a cutlery falls from the meal table, or when they receive an unexpected visit. The Lord Jesus warns us that on the Day of Judgment we will be judged for all the useless words we utter.[116]

The fifth commandment commands the keeping of one day a week, specifically the Sabbath day, for rest.

According to Exodus 20:11, God blessed and sanctified the Sabbath, because it was his day of rest after the creation of the heavens and the earth, and the number seven frequently appears in the biblical accounts, remembering that no number see power in numbers, which also translates into idolatry. possesses magical power for God. Only the occult

The book of Acts records that the first Christianity used to meet on the first day of the week, so it became a special day of worship and probably also of rest.

We read in the Larousse Cultural Encyclopedia, p. 1960, the opinion that the first day of the week (Sunday) replaced the Jewish Sabbath as the Lord's day, more for political injunctions than for any religious motivation, being that, from the 13th century onwards, "it became the object of a prescription (obligation to attend mass and general rest)".

The Apostle Paul held that Gentile Christians should not be censured for failing to guard the Sabbaths.[117]

Jesus taught that the Sabbath rest was instituted in function of man and not the Sabbath in function of man, making clear that the keeping of the seventh day is aimed at the rest of the person for his physical and mental recovery after a week of work; Hence this ordering does not prevent the provision of necessary or urgent services, such as performing cures work to obtain the livelihood of the day, priestly service, saving of person or animals and basic and vital care of animals.[118] [119] [120] [121] [122] [123]

To emphasize the hypocrisy of his accusers, Jesus taught that if they could care for their animals to have water on the Sabbath; Thus, He too could, with much more reason, free people from disease on that day.[124]

In another passage, we see Jesus teaching that healing on the Sabbath does not transgress the fifth commandment, just as the accomplishment of circumcision did not violate it either:

> "Jesus took up the word and said to them, 'I have only done one work', and you are all amazed. Moses gave you circumcision - although it comes from the patriarchs and not from Moses - and you practice it on the Sabbath day, without the law of Moses being broken, why be angry with me because I have completely healed a man on a Sabbath day? Cease to judge according to the appearance, learn to judge according to the righteous." (John 7:21-24).

It is interesting to note that although Jesus was Lord of the Sabbath (according to Matthew 12:5 and Luke 6:5), He always justified His acts biblically before His accusers, in this case, "the force of necessity" Demonstrating that the commandment was not being disregarded, as occurred when he recalled that King David and his companions, by necessity, used the showbread, although it was intended exclusively for priests.

For most people, it is not possible to guard the Saturday day, because the so-called English week - adopted in our legislation - came to require part-time work on Saturday day for most of the workers. The important thing, in this case, is that one day a week is saved for rest.

We must remember that God's will is directed that Christianity be practiced throughout the week, for our body is the temple of the Holy Spirit. In the book of Psalms, we read the following passage: "I hate and abhor falsehood, but I love your law. Seven times a day I praise you for your righteous ordinances." (Psalm 119:163-164, Bible Version of NIV Studies.)

There is no point in consecrating a day to worship and worship God if, for the rest of the week, we do not give the honors due to Him. Thus the Psalmist praises God seven times every day. Let us remember that the number 7 is associated with perfection and eternity. Therefore, according to the note found in the NIV Studies Bible, it is the "number that means a full account - it praises God all day long".

According to the teaching of Jesus, rest is important in itself, because the commandment was instituted in function of man, and this rest may occur on another day, since the divine commandment was intended to provide the physical and mental recovery of the person.

If, however, the Christian has a guilty conscience, he should reserve the Sabbath day for rest, because this will be pleasing to God. He will be honoring God by setting aside the Sabbath for his rest. Thus, both parts of Christendom cannot be blamed for not keeping the Sabbath, nor, in the same measure, should they be censured because they want to give this honor to God. the other part of Christianity that guards it,

Jesus, however, said that the Sabbath is not included in the moral ordinances of God, that is, in the commandments that translate the character of God (for example, not giving false testimony translates the character of God to always tell the truth)Seeing that the Son of God hath taught that the most

High worketh on the sabbath day: the commandment was instituted only for the benefit of man.

The Adventist church must not be identified by defending the keeping of the Sabbath, but by proclaiming the gospel of Jesus, the Christ. The Sabbath commandment should never be used as a banner to increase or decrease the ranks of churches, because the focus of every Christian church should be the proclamation of the gospel of Jesus, the Christ.

The sixth commandment is one of two commandments containing blessings. God grants prolonged life to those who honor and - as Leviticus 19:3 - fear their parents. God himself reserves for himself the treatment of the Father, as, for example, in the prayer of the Our Father, because He created us and loves us with fatherly love. [125]

The severity of the sin against the parents can be assessed by the appreciation of the punishment that was intended by the Mosaic law for the child who had insulted his parents. The punishment was the death of his son.[126]

Honor is more than just respect. To respect, according to the Great Encyclopedia Larousse Cultural, 20th volume, is to treat someone in a way that does not harm him, considering him as similar. Honoring someone means treating them with distinction, as if they were rising to a higher level. At a party, for example, we can respect all attendees, but an honor is only conferred on someone very special.

Caring for old parents, therefore, cannot be seen as a burden, but as an honor for the child. No reason justifies, in the eyes of God, the disregard of parents. No child can justify himself before God if he disrespects his parents, either because of their frailty, or because they are less literate, or because of the religious, political and economic convictions that parents profess.

God has granted authority to parents in relation to their children. Just as we relate in an affectionate way with our neighbors, with our friends and with our co-workers, we must treat and care for our parents with the same affection and with all the nobility of our heart and, for this, we must learn to forgivetruly and maintain a good and constant dialogue.

The seventh commandment contains the prohibition of murder. Murder can take away the victim's chance of salvation.

It's one of the gravest sins. By the law given to Moses, the murderer was to be put on trial and put to death if it was shown, through the testimony of more than one witness, that the act was done voluntarily. During the trial, the accused could take refuge in one of the six cities where he would be safe from the avengers of the dead, as reported in the book of Numbers 35:11 onwards.

God dwelt among the Jewish people, in the tabernacle. Murder profaned the land where God dwelt and He could not be indifferent or indulge in this profanation. And God said, "Ye shall not make the land wherein ye dwell, and in the midst of which I dwell, unclean. For I, Yahweh, dwell among the children of Israel." (Numbers 35:33-34)

The severity of the penalties imposed was justified, primarily, by the preservation of the holiness of the land where the Living God dwelt (tabernacle and adjacencies). This was a condition for God to continue to dwell in that land: that of not being profaned. It was also a need for his people to preserve their purity and holiness in order to continue to share God's presence.

Continuing the study of the commandments, we find adultery. It was God who conceived and instituted the union between man and woman, to which the human being gave a juridical garment and called it marriage.

When the couple pledges their word of mutual fidelity in marriage, he should not break it because of two motives. The first of these is that man and woman become one flesh according to the words of Jesus, the second is that God wants the relationship between woman and man to be authentic and this sanctifies it.[127]

Just as man corresponds to the glory of God in a relationship based on fidelity, so woman appears to be the glory of man based also on mutual fidelity in all respects.[128]

The seventh commandment forbids theft. Man must obtain the bread of his work, and never subtract goods from others. [129]

The eighth commandment prohibits kidnapping. According to the "d" commentary contained in the Bible, Ecumenical Translation, this commandment prohibits "taking over people to reduce them to slavery; would thus aim at any alienation from the freedom of others".

The ninth commandment deals with false testimony. The testimony has serious consequences for the life of the person you are testifying about. The testimony can lead the accused to death in the countries where this penalty is admitted, as was the case in the Mosaic era. The testimony is not only a statement made before a judge, but it is all assertive made in an informal group.

The book of Psalms contains a beautiful passage on the importance of refraining from forming groups of people to curse others: "Blessed is the man that walketh not in the counsel of the wicked, nor standeth in the way of sinners, nor sitteth in the seat of the scornful. But his delight is in the law of the LORD, and in his law he meditates day and night. He is like a tree planted by the stream of water, which in due season bringeth forth its fruit, and whose foliage fadeth not: and everything he does will be successful."[130]

The tenth commandment states that we should not covet the neighbor's goods, nor desire his wife, nor any thing that belongs to him. To covet something means to desire to take for oneself something belonging to one's neighbor.

The Bible tells of a sad example of the lust of another's wife, adultery and facilitation of murder. When King David had fallen in love with a married woman named Bathsheba, he lay with her and made her pregnant. To provoke the death of Uriah, her husband, David wrote to the commander of the army where Uriah was serving, and determined to put him in front of the greatest fighting force. This was done, which led to Uriah's death. David was forgiven by God (2 Samuel 12:13), but the son of adultery did not avenge.

The commandments of Exodus 20 were refreshed and enlarged as recorded in Chapter 34.

In this renewal, the Lord God commands the Jews not to defile themselves with the impurities and false gods of other peoples. Some commandments are reiterated and God commands the following: 1) the observance of certain feasts, which are: Unleavened of Weeks, of the harvest at the passage of the year, and the first fruits of the wheat harvest; 2) the appearance before God three times a year of every Jewish man; 3) It is reserved for God for all the firstborn of sheep and cattle.

The Lord spoke of other opportunities to the people of Israel, forbidding homosexuality, sexual relations with the wife of a countryman, sexual union with relatives and the like, sexual relations with a woman, betrothed or engaged in sexual intercourse with animals. In the case of flagrant sexual intercourse of a virgin woman who was not a bride, the man should take her as his wife throughout her life (Deuteronomy 22:29). [131] [132] [133] [134] [135]

other prohibitions: wage delay, prostitution, kidnapping, lying, falsehood against a countryman and the false oath in the name of God, shaving of the beard on the sides, rounding of the hair, tattoos and incisions on the body due to mourning; the defloration of a virgin woman; the eating with blood, the disrespect to the elderly (elders), and the use of scales and incorrect measures in disagreement with the regulations.[136][137][138][139][140][141]

This corresponds to the general panorama of the law as brought to us by the Holy and Ancient Scriptures, whose knowledge will serve as a background for the study of the commandments of Jesus of Nazareth and the steps to an abundant life.

4 *The commandments in the teaching of Jesus*

One of the many times that Jesus' authority was tested, a Pharisee asked him what the great commandment of the Law was. The Pharisee wanted to put Jesus in difficulty before the doctors of the Law and Jewish leaders, asking him a question that involved a controversial and complex subject.

Judaism was in a process of permanent detailing of the law: it started from the laws granted by God contained in the Pentateuch (Torah) and in the books of the Prophets, which were considered as fundamental principles and were made additions and extensive interpretations, the details of any unlawful conduct. In the third century, a condensation was made of the oral interpretations of the law, which was called the Mishnah, composed of 63 treatises. The *Talmud* consists of the commentary of the Mishnah *and consists* of 12 volumes, of which the Babylonian one consists of 60 volumes.

To get an idea of the entanglement of additions that were made to the law, it was interpreted that the fourth commandment .(Keeping of the Sabbath) prohibited carrying "a burden", arriving at the minutiae of conceiving it as "the weight equal to a dried fig, ink enough to write two letters, oil enough to anoint a wound" etc., as explained by Pastor Nilson Fanini[142]

David sought to condense the law and proposed 11 precepts that should be followed by those who desire to dwell in heaven. Then Isaiah highlighted six recommendations. Micah proposed to summarize the law in three precepts: 1st) the practice [143][144][145]of justice; 2nd) the benefit of charity; 3rd) walk with God with humility. Habakkuk established the principle that "the just shall live by his faith".[146]

Jesus answered the Pharisee, quoting not one but two commandments, on which all the law and the prophets depend, according to the constant passage in Matthew 22:34 to 40:

> "The Pharisees, hearing that he had shut the mouth of the Sadducees, gathered together and one of them - in order to test him - asked him: Master, what is the great commandment of the Law? And he said, Thou shalt love the Lord thy God with all thy heart, and with all thy soul, and with all thy mind. That is the great first commandment. The second is like unto him, Thou shalt love thy neighbour as thyself. On

<blockquote>these two commandments hang all the Law and the Prophets."</blockquote>

The solution given by God the Son was admirable: it summed up the whole law and the prophets in only two great commandments, teaching that the love of God above all things is in the beginning of all obedience and that only by loving one another can we please the Lord. [147]

The main question - which soon comes to mind - is to understand the extent to which the two great commandments taught by Jesus replace the whole law.

First, let us examine the Master's own words: "On these two commandments hang all the law and the prophets." Therefore, put another way, the full fulfillment of the law depends on loving God above all things and loving your neighbor as yourself.

When one thing is dependent on the other, this does not mean exclusion from that which is dependent: the two coexist, but there is a cause and effect relationship between them.

Likewise, the principles mentioned by Jesus do not replace the prohibitions that are detailed in the Word of God. One does not exclude the other. They complement each other at the level of cause and effect. The principle only draws from the detail what is common to the whole order.

Jesus said that when we are moved by love, we can do things that are pleasing to God and to our neighbor. Love is the basis of the fulfillment of every divine law.

When we behave before God and our fellow men as the Word of God teaches us, we are loving the Most High and our neighbor.

There is no other way to love the Most High and neighbour than to interpret the situations of life, making use of the lens of the Word of God, which is the divine reference for us.

The Bible teaches us how, when, and how we can love the Most High and our fellows.

This love has a supernatural nature and, by far, it is not the love celebrated by society. We live in a time of free love in all aspects where every kind of prohibition is seen as prejudice. Today, the children are above the parents and it is the parents who usually live according to the whims of the children. The Bible, however, is very clear in disapproving of homosexual and out-of-wedlock sexual intercourse, as well as stipulating that children should respect parents, regardless of what they say or do.

And what about love to the enemy? This is a commandment of Jesus totally incomprehensible to humanity, for which only the weak do not react to the height, overthrowing and eliminating their enemies.

These are just a few examples of the difference between biblical love and the love that humanity knows.

The Word of God is the compass that points to the true north.

Jesus taught that the Jews did well to examine the Scriptures, stating that they were wrong not to know them and that the love devoted to Him was measured by the commitment of His disciples to keep His commandments.[148][149][150]

The commandments of love represent more the mode and form (principle) than the content (detailing behavior). Love consists of an altruistic and noble feeling, which makes us wish the best for the loved one.

The difficulty arises when we try to define what is best for our fellow man. We may want good things for the other person, but we may be completely and sincerely wrong about what is best for them.

Often the best in our understanding does not correspond to the best as seen by God.

Is the best thing for our kids a fat bank account, a good marriage, or the car of the year? All these things are good and can be true blessings from heaven.

We have already wondered if our children have received the most important blessing of all, which is to have received Jesus. According to the Word of God, this grace, no doubt, is the supernumption of the best for our children and for anyone.

The best thing for anyone is to achieve salvation and Jesus has designated us as co-participants in the work of the Holy Spirit, and it is up to Christians to show an exemplary and different life based on the supernatural love of God.

If we truly love our neighbor, we will be occupied with his spiritual guidance and desire to share eternity with him.

It is this love that will pave the way opened by testimony. To speak one thing and live another is a more nefarious hypocrisy than that of the Pharisees, who did not believe in the Nazarene.

The Bible does not support the interpretation that the two great commandments, spoken by Jesus, were replacing the other divine precepts.

He who loves God seeks to know and fulfill his will so that a lasting and pleasant relationship may be maintained between them. So also he who loves his neighbor, seeks to know him and become aware of the situation in which he finds himself, involving himself in his life and helping him if necessary. We can only please God and demonstrate true love if we know His Word and His will for our lives.

The Most High does not present himself as an unknown. God has made known to us by His Word and much of the character of God has been revealed to us by the life of Jesus, since God the Father and Jesus Christ are one in His purposes and His will. [151][152][153]

The Most High is the same as yesterday, today and his Word always reveals to us all that we must know about his character, his will in relation to human coexistence and the way to worship him, there being nothing hidden or mysterious in these points. [154]

Because God is not unknown, we can be sure that the way to worship him and to keep fidelity to Him, as well as the way He wants the coexistence between people to be established, is reported in detail in the Holy Scriptures and that is the north that should be very clear to every Christian.

Jesus Himself made it clear that He did not come to "revoke the law and the prophets... but to give them full fulfillment" (Matthew 5:17).

It is thus understood in principle that all divine precepts, including those in the Old Testament, continue to govern the life of the Christian. When we refer to the law and the prophets, we are not including what is called the ceremonial law, that is, the Jewish interpretations of the law, the Jewish customs or festivals and traditions, which are part of the specific Jewish culture.

The moral or essential law remains, that is, the part that understands the precepts of personal conduct and human coexistence that reflect the person of God and his values and that must result from the love we feel for the Most High and for our neighbour.

According to Proverbs, God's law is meant to instruct man, and God desires that his precepts be the apple of our eyes and that we write them on the tablet of our hearts.[155][156]

The two commandments - quoted by Jesus - are found in the Old Testament as transcribed below. The novelty of Jesus' teaching lies in the fact that they were raised to commandments of greater importance, precisely because they contain the principles on which the fulfillment of the whole law depends.

> "Hear, O Israel: Iahweh our God is the only Iahweh! Therefore, Thou shalt come to Iahweh thy God with all thy heart, and with all thy soul, and with all thy strength. May these words that I command you today be in your heart! You will teach them to your children, and you will speak of them sitting in your house and walking in your way, lying down and standing." (Deuteronomy 6:4-7)

"Thou shalt not have hatred in thy heart for thy brother. You must rebuke your neighbor, and so you shall not be guilty of sin. You shall not avenge yourself, nor bear a grudge against the children of your people. You will love your neighbor as yourself. I am Iahweh." (Leviticus 19:18)

The two great commandments are the principles that inform all the precepts of the law. Whoever loves God above all things will want to know the will of God and conform his behavior to divine precepts. Likewise, whoever loves his neighbor as himself will not harm him.

It is interesting that, with the new approach given by Jesus in emphasizing the principles of what we can do, the way of enunciating the commandments by means of prohibitions loses force, while the law of love gains body: permission to love our neighbor as ourselves and God above all things.

We are sure that the two great commandments - emphasized by Jesus - do not replace the other divine precepts, but complete them and enable them to be fulfilled, because loving God implies seeking to attend to His will and please Him; This relates directly to the fulfillment of the biblical precepts, which give us the direction to follow in each circumstance.

Thus, loving God means adopting postures and behaviors in our life that are in accordance with divine precepts. [157][158]

Jesus reasoned in this regard as follows:

> "Think not that I am come to destroy the law, or the prophets: I am not come to destroy, but to fulfill. For verily I say unto you, Before heaven and earth pass, an i or a dot of i shall not pass [159]f[160]rom *the* law, till all be fulfilled. Therefore, in the kingdom of heaven, whosoever shall transgress one of these least commandments, and teach men to do the same, shall be declared the least; On the contrary, whoever puts them into practice and teaches them, in the kingdom of heaven will be declared great." (Matthew 5:17 to 19, BTE)

Understanding that the Christian is subject to the fulfillment of the Scriptures as a whole, what is different about the good news of Jesus? This difference lies in the fact that the Christian receives divine presence and help, which is covered in more detail in the topic "Sanctifying Himself". [161]

To reinforce the argument that there was no repeal of the law, we read the biblical passage that narrates the episode in which a rich man, of remarkable position, heard from Jesus what he should do to inherit eternal life:

> "You know the commandments, Do not commit adultery, do not kill, do not steal, do not bear false witness; honor your father and your mother". When the man said that he observed all this, the Lord Jesus answered, "There is one thing still missing from you. Sell all that thou hast, and distribute unto the poor, and thou shalt have treasure in heaven: Then come and follow me." [162]

Jesus stresses that the commandments must be known and observed for salvation and that the heavenly reward of that man would be to sell his goods and follow him. [163]

Jesus determined some notable changes in relation to the law, invested with all the authority to do so, alongside the authority to heal, to cast out demons, and to remit and forgive sins". [164]

> "When they saw him, they fell down, but some had doubts. Jesus approached them and said these words: "**All authority has been given to Me in heaven and on earth" (Matthew** 28:17-18, BTE; highlights are not in the source text.)

> He who comes from above is above all. He that is of the earth is earthly, and speaketh on the earth. He that cometh from heaven beareth witness of him that hath seen, and of him that hath heard, and no man receiveth his testimony. He who receives his testimony

confirms that God is true. For he whom God has sent says the words of God, which the Spirit gives him without measure. **The Father loves the Son and has given everything into his hand.** He who believes in the Son has eternal life; He that refuseth to believe on the Son shall not see life, but the wrath of God abideth upon him." (John 3:31 to 36, BTE; highlights are not in the source text.).

Two of these changes were so profound that they transformed the impositions that the law made to the Jews into precepts of justice, faithfulness, and mercy **according** to **the teaching** of **Jesus.**[165]

The first major change promoted by Jesus was to disallow the Jewish people and leaders to judge and condemn their fellow men by punishing them on the basis of the commandments of God and on his behalf.

Going back in history, we find Moses receiving from God the ordinances addressed to the Jewish people, which were endowed with sanctions of a preventive nature.

The Mosaic law, like every law, contained sanctions for the transgression of the precept, which could not pass from the sinful person. The penalties were varied: one spit; a maximum of 40 lashes; amputation of the hands; may reach the death penalty by stoning; this, provided for in not a few situations, as, for example, in case of insult against parents.[166] [167] [168] [169] [170]

The sanctions were intended to inhibit lawlessness and maintain the holiness of the people and the tabernacle where the Most High dwelt.

Jesus abolished the sanctions because obedience must spring from people's hearts and not as a result of fear, having disallowed the condemnation among fellow men, since we are all sinners.

With the maxim: "Do not set yourselves up as judges, lest you be judged," Jesus disallowed those who would later be called Christians, of judging and condemning their fellow man, having remained from the Jewish power only the duty of reproof among believers, although the apostle Paul also includes the penalty of separation from living together.[171] [172] [173]

The trial and the sanction were part of the garment inherent in the law. The law was to be observed and enforced by all, and for this it was enforced by force, that is, it was endowed with mechanisms of coercion (sanction), which had to be applied immediately and vigorously, so that respect for the law was enforced effectively.

While the Mosaic law aimed at the sanctification of a people as a whole - through preventive and other sanctions of a segregating nature -, Jesus came into the world to allow sinners to return to God's fold and be sanctified by the experience of being born again. From Jesus, there was no more exclusion from coexistence or elimination in the communities. Jesus, moreover, had already foreseen the coexistence between the holy (wheat) and the unclean (tares) within the communities that would be formed. The Invisible Church of Christ comprises saved believers, regardless of religious denomination; while the church constitutes a human body, or institution. [174]

The second change, announced by Jesus in the structure of the first covenant, concerned the fact that true believers would not be judged, but would pass from death to eternal life. Thus whoever is saved and perseveres to the end will not be judged, since, having been approved by God at the time of conversion, he remained faithful to the end. [175]

With these two profound changes in the legislative and judicious structure of the first alliance, what is left of the law? Indeed, what was left of the law was so weakened that it could no longer be called the law as we know it, but it arose, for new believers, as precepts of justice, mercy (love) and faithfulness, observed spontaneously with the help of God.

This subject will be taken up in the Chapter "Sanctifying Oneself" to understand the terminology employed by Paul (law and justice).

Jesus also brought other substantial novelties as happened in relation to precepts of taking vows to God, or swearing. The Most High determined that any vows rendered to Him should be fulfilled:

> "If thou vow a vow unto the LORD thy God, delay not to do it: for otherwise the LORD thy God would not cease to claim it of thee, which is a sin upon thee. But if you renounce vows, it will not be a sin to you. That which proceedeth out of thy lips, take heed to put it into effect, according to the spontaneous vow unto the LORD thy God, which thou hast uttered with thy mouth." (Deuteronomy 23:22-24, BTE)

And Moses spake unto the children of Israel all that the LORD commanded him. Moses spoke to the heads of the tribes of the children of Israel:

> "This is the commandment which the LORD hath given: If a man vow a vow unto the LORD, or hath made a vow unto himself under an oath, he shall not break his word: he shall act according to the very thing that proceedeth out of his mouth." (Numbers 30:3, BTE).

Jesus, however, forbade the vow to God under any circumstances, as read in Matthew 5:

> "And ye have heard what was spoken unto the ancients, saying, Thou shalt not swear, but perform thy oaths unto the Lord. But I say unto you, Swear not at all: neither by heaven which is the throne of God, nor by the earth which is the footstool of his feet, nor by Jerusalem which is the city of the great King. Don't swear on your head either, for you can't make one hair turn white or black. When you speak, say 'Yes' or 'No': all the rest comes from the evil one." (Matthew 5:33 to 37, BTE)

This is a typical example of Jesus' new commandment. At the time of Jesus, the law was interpreted in the sense that, in principle, one should not take an oath, but if one were to do so for some serious reason, one should do so. However, Jesus strictly forbade vows or oaths in any circumstances; teaching that is in accordance with the commandment not to take the name of God in vain (Exodus 20:7). Jesus also teaches that Jesus does not teach us that "let it be your yes, yes, and your no, no. What comes of this comes from the Evil One." We should even swear by ourselves (by our heads), since we do not have "the power to make one hair white or black" (Matthew 5:36). Therefore, it is evident that, with much more reason, we should not swear by the name of God, because we have no complete control over all the circumstances surrounding the fact about which the oath was taken. [176]

Swearing an oath or vow to God on condition of receiving something in return constitutes a typical language of antifé. When something is asked of God legitimately and with faith, the Most High graciously grants it, if it is in his will.

Even in relation to the commandment of love of neighbour, Jesus brought profound changes.

The Jews understood the commandment to love one's neighbor as the fraternal feeling that strengthened the bonds of the Jewish community. Jesus, however, went deeper and taught that love must break the circle of the community, that is, it is not enough to just love people who share the same ideals, beliefs and blood ties.

When Jesus taught whom the Jew should address the noble sentiment, he told the parable of the Good Samaritan.[177]

Consider the reader that Jesus spoke to Jews, who had the privilege of directly witnessing his ministry as it appears from the text in Matthew 10:6, when the disciples are sent, preferably, "to the lost sheep of the house of Israel" (BTE)Differentiating them from the Samaritans and the Gentiles. Therefore, Jesus could not have better illustrated the notion of "neighbor" to the Jews, who were the audience to whom the message was originally addressed, so that it would be evident that the feeling should exceed the community boundaries.[178]

But Jesus did not stop there. He taught that we should love our enemies, greet them, and pray for them.[179]

It could not be more appropriate - to the public of the time - the illustration that Jesus made about the notion of neighbor, so that one could understand the extent of the love that God expects of believers. Thus, this aspect is fully elucidated through the parable of the Good Samaritan, extending the notion of who belonged to a people considered an enemy of the Jews.

According to John L. Mckenzie, "Samaritans is the name given to the inhabitants of the district of Samaria... To the Jews, the Samaritans were a heretical and schismatic group of spurious worshippers of the God of Israel, detested, even more than the pagans... The Jews who settled in Jerusalem after the edict of Cyrus (. c.) did not regard the community that dwelt in the district of Samaria, and ancient center of Israel, as true Israelites. They were the descendants of a mixed population: Israelites who had survived the Assyrian deportations and populations of various Mesopotamian communities who had been transferred to Israel".[180]538 a[181]

Jesus enunciated new commandments and mitigated or softened others (regarding the Sabbath and law on unclean foods); But in general his reading of the law not only confirmed its efficacy and validity, but drew from it all the rigour of the commandments, giving it a reach which the doctors of the law did not lend him. [182][183]

This rigor appears, for example, when Jesus attributes the sin of adultery to anyone who looks at a woman with an unclean intention.[184]

He also teaches us that God is a loving Father, but also clarifies that God is a severe Lord, as is easily extracted from the parable of the mines and many others of his lectures, as the warnings that we will be judged by the useless words we utter and the one we find in the gospel of Matthew:[185][186]

> "I assure you that if your righteousness does not exceed that of the scribes and the Pharisees, you will not enter the kingdom of heaven. Ye have heard that it was said unto the ancients, Thou shalt not kill; And he that killeth must answer, but I say unto you, Whosoever will be angry with his brother shall answer in judgment: Whosoever shall call his brother a cretin! shall be subject to the judgment of the Sanhedrin; He who calls him a fool will have to answer the judgment of the Fiery Sea." (Matthew 5:20 to 22). em juízo. Eu

Moreover, in the following verses of Matthew five, the Lord Jesus criticizes the interpretation of the scribes and Pharisees, sometimes mild and permissive, and at other times modifying the commandments of God, in relation to the following biblical precepts and recommendations: prohibition of adultery; permission to divorce in case of repudiation; retribution of the damage by the equivalent ("eye for eye" and "tooth for tooth") and hatred of enemies.[187] [188] [189] [190]

Jesus, when talking about the precepts linked to the "eye for eye" and "tooth for tooth", left us this beautiful passage:

> "Ye have heard what was said, An eye for an eye and a tooth for a tooth. But I say unto you, Resist not the wicked. On the contrary, if someone slaps you on the right cheek, turn the other cheek too. Whosoever will lead thee before the judge to take thy garment, give him also thy mantle. If any man compel thee to go a thousand paces, let him walk with him two thousand. Give to him that asketh thee: Don't turn away from him who wants to borrow you." (Matthew 5:38-42).

But let us remember that the zeal of Jesus for the things of God determined his reaction against the sellers and the money changers who traded in the Temple of Jerusalem.Indeed, the life of Jesus is not the emblem of zeal for the things of his Father: he always spoke, to openly denounce the hypocrisy and bad example of the religious leaders of the time, while at the same time their life reflects a perfect example that the believer applies to follow. [191]

The old precept of reparation of the damage by the equivalent had a markedly preventive character: it instituted a retribution as serious as the one that wanted to avoid, discouraging the action that was condemned by the law. Most likely, such reparations were instituted because of the hardness of the heart of the Israelites, similar to the precept that made possible the repudiation of the wife.[192]

It is wrong to think that the law allowed private vengeance, that is, that the retribution of the damage that could reach death, would be justified by the satisfaction of a passionate feeling of the person who felt "harmed", and not by the sanctification of the place and the Jewish people, as a requirement of God that he might dwell among the people and that they might share his presence. It was never the will of God to institute private vengeance, or to attribute to man the "right" to eliminate whomever he pleased.

Circumcision was instituted also for the identification of the Jewish people, and there was no reason for it to be extended to non-Jews who converted to Christianity, who publicly demonstrate their faith by baptism.[193]

Another major change recommended by Jesus concerns food, as interpreted in the biblical passage cited below:

> "There is nothing outward to a man that by entering him can make him unclean, but what comes out of a man, this is what makes a man unclean." After he entered the house, far from the crowd, his disciples questioned him about this enigmatic word. He said to them, "Are you also without intelligence? Know ye not that nothing that entereth into man from without can make him unclean, inasmuch as it entereth not into his heart, but into his belly, and goeth into the pit?" With this, he declared that all food is pure. He said, "What comes out of a man, that makes a man unclean. Indeed, it is from within, it is from the heart of man that come forth evil intentions, disorders, thefts, murders, adulteries, greed, wickedness, cunning, envy, insults, vanity, foolishness. All this evil comes from within and makes man unclean." (BTE, Mark 7:15 to 23).

The Apostle Peter, who was a Jew, had to witness, repeatedly, a divine vision that commanded him to eat foods considered unclean by Judaism, to understand that they had been cleansed by those who had and have the authority to do so, the very Son of God. [194]

If the Christian, however, in the same way as the Sabbath commandment, feels his conscience heavy while eating pork, he will be honoring God if he deprives himself of this food.

With the universalization of Christianity, the need arose to define for Christianity in general what precepts the Gentiles should obey. [195]

This prompted Peter to deliver a speech at Jerusalem to resolve the controversy raised by the scribes, converts to Christianity, who held that Gentiles should also observe some Jewish precepts and traditions. Peter spoke and said:

> "Brethren, ye know that from the first days God chose me from among you, that the Gentiles should hear the word of the gospel from my mouth, and should open their faith. And God, who knows the hearts, testified in their behalf, giving them the Holy Spirit as to us. He made no distinction between them and us, for he purified their hearts by faith. Why do ye now tempt God, to impose upon the disciples a yoke which neither your fathers nor we had the strength to bear? Indeed, it is by the grace of the Lord Jesus that we believe we are saved, just like them."[196]

Thus the leaders, in the so-called Jerusalem Council, commanded that the Gentile converts should abstain from what was contaminated by idols, illegitimate unions, suffocated flesh, and blood (Acts 15:20). As for circumcision, the leaders also came to the conclusion that the ritual could not be imposed on believers who were not Jews.

Consider, however, that, surely, Jesus never ate food considered unclean by the Law. Peter, who was one of his closest disciples, had never eaten unclean food, and did so secondary to the Master.

We record Flusser's opinion as to the survival of the precept concerning food for the Jew who, in his conception, "takes his Judaism seriously": [197]

> "it was God's will that Christianity spread westward to Europe. Christianity therefore penetrated the Greco-Roman world, later becoming a European religion. In contrast to the cultural environment of Judaism and the religions of East Asia, beginning in Persia, Western culture has contributed to Christianity's disenchantment of ritual or ceremonial precepts as regards various foods, drinks and ablutions.' (Heb 9:10). According to the European view, it is permissible to eat everything that is sold on the market, without raising doubts for reasons of conscience. For

> the earth and all that it contains belongs to the
> Lord (I Cor. 10:25-26)."

Bear in mind that Jesus came to announce salvation first to the Jews, and Jesus was not busy proposing a rule that would encompass future Gentile believers.

For Flusser, Jesus was a "Jew faithful to the Law, who had never had to face the need to adapt his Judaism to the European way of life. For Jesus there was, of course, the peculiar problem of his relation to the Law and its precepts".[198]

It should be noted that the conclusion of the leaders of the Early Church aimed at the reception of the Gentiles to the fellowship of the Christian community, not being in any way the complete statement of a doctrine that would be opposed to the teaching of Jesus.

It cannot be interpreted that the conclusion of the Christian leaders was freeing the Gentiles from all their sins. Could then the Gentiles bear false witness? Of course you don't!

Indeed, these discussions in the Early Church had as a background the subsistence of Jewish traditions and rituals (ceremonial law), because no doubt could remain regarding the law and the prophets (moral law), excepting, of course, the precepts that were revoked or modified by Jesus, or those that lost their purpose at the advent of the second covenant (ceremonial law and prescriptions regarding purification).

It is important to distinguish what are the law and the prophets (God's moral law) and what are commentaries of the learned and tradition. The law composes the prescriptions directly granted by God; the Jewish traditions are the customs and customs consecrated by their reiteration, whose observance came to be considered obligatory among the Jews, but it was not always in accordance with the law.

This is the case, for example, of the Corban tradition. According to him, the Jew could fail to give assistance to his parents if their property were consecrated to God. The Lord Jesus harshly criticized this tradition. When the Pharisees and scribes criticized Jesus and his disciples for not washing their hands before eating, Jesus answered them: [199]

> "And why do you violate the commandment of God because of your tradition? In fact, God said, Honor thy father and mother, and he that curseth father or mother shall surely die." But you say, "Whosoever shall say unto his father or

> to his mother, that which thou mightest receive of me is consecrated unto God; he is not bound to honour his father or mother. And so you invalidated the Word of God because of your tradition."[200]

The apostle Paul also held that the Christian should not be censured for the lack of observance of traditions, such as Jewish feasts and holidays and the new moon ceremonies.[201]

Though not obligatory, for it was not a commandment, the logical thing would be for the Jewish Christians to observe these traditions, for many of them were instituted by God Himself, according to Exodus 34, as the feast of Unleavened Bread, of the Weeks, the First Fruits of the Wheat Harvest and the Harvest Festival on the New Year. The observance of these festivities was ordered to the Jewish people, so that they would never forget some special episodes of the history of this People in their walk with God, such as the liberation from Egypt. [202]

We can conclude by saying that Christians are under the law of grace and this empowers and impels them **to** the spontaneous **and** sincere fulfillment of the divine commandments.

5 *The remission of sins and deliverance from the power of sin*

5.1 *The atonement for sins in the first covenant*

The great miracles performed by God and the suffering through which the Jewish people spent the 40 years - in which they crossed the desert to the Promised Land (Canaan, later called Israel) - were unfortunately not enough to break up this magnificent people, but undoubtedly recalcitrant. Although he worshipped God through formal rituals, many of them instituted by the Mosaic Law, most of the Jews, as the Bible tells us, did not worship him with their hearts and minds.

Since the children of Adam, we have heard that man made offerings to God as a sign of repentance for sins. The first two sons of Adam were named Cain and Abel. While Cain was cultivating the soil, Abel was herding sheep. Once, Abel offered to God the firstfruits and the fat of his flock, and Cain presented the fruits of his labour on the ground. [203]

The Bible reports that God was pleased only with Abel's offering, not by the nature or quality of the offering, but by the fact that Cain was motivated by the spirit of competition and not by the desire to please God. Cain was enraged and his face was upset because Abel's offering had been accepted.

After the exodus from Egypt, God appointed the brother of Moses, Aaron, and his sons, as high priests, It was up to the high priests to perform the rituals concerning the tabernacle, among which was the immolation, Or the sacrifice of beasts without blemish for the atonement of their own sins, and of all the people. God, in witnessing the sacrifice of animals and the sprinkling of their blood, forgave the sins of the one who offered the sacrifice as a sign of his repentance.[204]

God determined for Moses and Aaron that a special day be instituted in the calendar: the day of atonement (Leviticus 16). On that day, the Blood was taken from the sin offering and brought to the Most Holy Place, where it was sprinkled seven times before the Lord. Although the offering was made . publicly, only the High Priest celebrated this ritual, making the intermediation between God and the people[205]

In another passage of the Bible, in Exodus 12:13, we find the sprinkling of the blood of the paschal lamb on the lintels and doorposts for the redemption of the Jews who were captive in Egypt, the Lord God having said that: "When I see the blood, I will pass over, and the scourge of destruction shall not be among you."[206]

Blood is essential to human life and to the life of animals. But the blood of sacrifice was a requirement of God for atonement for people's sins based on the symbolic valuation He makes of the blood in this process.

From the earliest times, God forbade man to feed on blood, because it corresponds to the life of the flesh. [207]

Despite the ritual of atonement for sins, the Bible reports that Israel departed from God: "The Lord said, Because this people draw nigh unto me, they honour me with their mouth and with their lips: but their heart is far from me, and their fear of me is but the commandments of men, which they have mechanised."[208]

God did not like the offerings, because they were not accompanied by sincerity as reported in the book of Micah:

> "How can we make up for the wrong we've done?" you ask. "Shall we bow before the Lord and bring as a year-old calf offering? No! If you offer the Lord thousands of rams and ten

thousand rivers of oil, will that please Him? Will He be satisfied? If you sacrifice the eldest son, will that make the Lord happy? Will He forgive your sins with all this? Of course you don't! No, He has already said what He desires and that is summed up in: to be honest and righteous, to know how to love and forgive, and to be humble before your God." (Micah 6:6 to 8)

Once Jesus warned his disciples and the multitudes to do what the Pharisees and the scribes said, but not what they did.

One should also consider the fact that, although offerings were effective for atoning for sins previously committed, they had no bearing on the principle of sin, or the power that led people to sin. That is, the offerings did not change the sinful nature, that is, they did not eliminate the principle that had triggered sin. Even after a confession, the human inclination to sin speaks louder than the spiritual nature and the relapse is certain, which brings, among other terrible consequences, the frustration that accompanies every person who sincerely seeks God.

So it is with any of us: while we deal only with our past sins without seeking a change in our old sinful constitution, we cannot please God with our own efforts **or merits, just as the**

valiant Jewish people failed to obey, to all the precepts of the Divine Law, with all my heart and with all my mind.

5.2   *The Second Covenant - Jesus, the High Priest*

From what we have been able to study, it is impossible - humanly speaking - to fully please and obey his enables the justification of all who seek him sincerely. God and with Him maintain fellowship, knowing that He requires a high degree of obedience and holiness, but the perfect plan

Because God, in his infinite mercy, established a second great covenant with Israel, which would later be extended to all mankind. God tells us about it in the Book of Jeremiah 31:31:[209]

> "Behold, the days come, saith the LORD, and I will make a new covenant with the house of Israel and with the house of Judah.
>
> 32. Not according to the covenant with their fathers in the day that I formed them by the hand to bring them out of the land of Egypt, because they have made my covenant void, because I had betrothed them, saith the LORD.

33. For this is the covenant that I will make with the house of Israel after those days, saith the LORD. **I will print my laws in their minds, I will write them also in their hearts; I will be their God, and they shall be my people.**

34. And they shall not teach every man his neighbour, nor every man his brother, saying, Know the LORD: for all shall know me, from the least even unto the greatest of them, saith the LORD. For I will forgive their iniquities, and their sins will I remember no more.

35. Thus saith the LORD that giveth the sun for the light of the day, and the laws of the moon and the stars for the light of the night, which shaketh the sea, and maketh the waves thereof to roar; The LORD of hosts is his name.

36. If these ordinances fail before me, saith the LORD, the seed of Israel also shall cease from being a nation before me for ever.

37. Thus saith the LORD; If heaven above can be measured, and the foundations of the earth searched out beneath, I will also cast off all the seed of Israel for all that they have done, saith the LORD. ...

40. ... This Jerusalem will never be uprooted or destroyed."

Well, this second covenant was instituted with the coming, death and resurrection of Jesus Christ, who lived the greatest love story between a merciful God and his creature.

At the time of the Tent of Meeting (first covenant), only the High Priest could, once a year (day of atonement), enter the Most Holy Place where the Lord God dwelt and which was behind the veil.[210][211]

The atonement was to be made "for the sanctuary, for the defilements of the children of Israel, for their transgressions, and for all their sins".[212]

The Apostle Paul, in the Epistle to the Hebrews (Chapter 9), addresses the Jews, speaking to them about the Tent of Meeting:

> "The first covenant had, in fact, a ritual for worship and an earthly temple. For he set himself in a tent: a first tent, called the Holy One, where the lampstand, the table, and the showbread were. Behind the second veil was another tabernacle, which is called the Most Holy, with the golden altar for perfumes, the ark of the covenant, all covered with gold, and in it a golden pot with manna, and the staff of Aaron that flourished, and the tables of the covenant; Above the ark the cherubim of glory covered the mercy seat with their shadow. However,

this is not the time to go into the details. Being so disposed, the priests enter at any time in the first tent, to perform the service of worship. In the second, however, only the high priest enters, and only once a year, and this does not happen without first offering blood for his faults and for those of the people. The Holy Spirit wanted to show, by this, that the way to the sanctuary is not opened as long as the first tent exists. There is in it a symbol for the time now. For in that diet there were offerings and sacrifices without efficacy to perfect the conscience of the worshiper. All were human rituals concerning food, drink, various ablations, imposed only until the time of correction." (Hebrews 9:1-10)

Jesus Christ, the Sent Son of God, assumed, in the second great covenant, the unique position **of** One Priest, in the mediation between God and men. It is only through him that legitimate Christians will be cleansed and saved as the apostle Paul explained:

"But Christ came as high priest of good things to come. He went through a bigger and more perfect tent, which is not the work of human hands, that is, which does not belong to this creation. He entered the Sanctuary once and for all, not with the blood of goats and calves, but with his own blood, obtaining eternal redemption. For if the blood of goats and bullocks, and the ashes of the heifer, scattered

upon the ritually unclean beings, sanctify them
by purifying their bodies, how much more the
blood of Christ, who by an eternal spirit offered
himself to God as a victim without spot, He will
cleanse our conscience from dead works, that
we may worship the living God." (Paul, Epistle
to Hebrews 9:11-14.)

I open a parenthesis to mention that in my next work
[God's conditional love (in) I will be dealing with other
categories of saved, such as the righteous, all in accordance
with the teaching of Master Jesus.

When Jesus gave up the spirit on Calvary, "the veil of the
Sanctuary was rent in two parts, from top to bottom, the earth
trembled and the rocks split". And in this, "the tombs were
opened and many bodies of the deceased saints were
resurrected". [213]

When the veil of the Sanctuary was torn, God began to
relate directly to the people who came to him as a result of
faith in Jesus Christ, who is the High Priest who allows this
mediation.

Hence the reason Jesus prophesied that the Temple
would be destroyed, and in three days he would raise it up. He

was not referring to the Temple as a human construction, but to Jesus the veil of the sanctuary came expiring, and the mediation was reestablished through the resurrection of Jesus Christ at the end of three days. new mediation between God and men that is made through his Person. The mediation between God and the High Priest was destroyed at the time [214]

Jesus, occupying the position of sole High Priest, is the center of our consideration of the remission of sins, which is why it is critical that you know Jesus better and understand why.

It is essential to know Jesus, his sovereignty and his investiture as the only High Priest. Many question, in their hearts, the basis of every gospel and even accept the divine nature (=from whom it came from God) and mediator of the singular and unique Jesus, the Christ (=Anointed; Salvador).

Of course, if these people had knowledge of the Scriptures and put their belief in them, they would never have this doubt, because the Scriptures lead to Jesus as the Messiah and God the Son Himself. But the evil of these people lies in their unbelief about the Word of God. [215]

Accepting as true the Holy Scriptures, one cannot fail to recognize that Jesus Christ is the Son of God partaker of the Heavenly Council, who, having stripped himself of all his kingship, came to earth in human form conceived by the virgin Mary and begotten by the Holy Spirit. [216] [217]

The divine nature of Jesus is recorded in the gospel of John:[218]

> "In the beginning was the word, and the word was with God, and the word was God. He was in the beginning with God. All things were made through him: and without him was not any thing made that was made. Life was in him, and life was the light of men. The light shines in the darkness, and the darkness has not prevailed against it."

Also Paul, in the Epistle to the Philippians, speaks of the divine nature of Jesus:

> "Let each one look not only for himself, but also for others. Behave among yourselves as you do ; He, who is of divine condition, did not regard it as a prey to grasp the equal being of God. But he stripped himself, becoming a servant, and made himself like men, and by his appearance acknowledged as man; He stooped down, becoming obedient unto death, and death on a cross. That is why God exalted him sovereignly

and gave him the Name which is above every name, that at the name of Jesus every knee should bow, in heaven, on earth, and under the earth, and every tongue should confess that Jesus Christ is Lord, to the glory of God the Father." (BTE, Philippians 2:4-11)em Jesus Cristo

Jesus is the light of the world and everything was made through Him and for Him, for He pre-existed creation. [219][220]

Harold Hill wrote brilliantly about Jesus' role in creation: [221]

"When Albert Einstein came up with his surprising discovery of the relationship between energy and matter, he was entirely in agreement with the creation account in the first part of Genesis. Relativity existed from the beginning, even before man appeared to invent science and mathematics.

At first, when Einstein presented his formula E = MC2 (= Energy equals mass times the speed of light squared), no one believed him...

However, as time went on, scientists began to learn more and more about how things really worked and, you see, they started scratching their heads saying:

- You know, I think Albert Einstein was very close. To tell you the truth, from what I've seen in the lab, what he says has to be true!

I can even imagine God laughing his ass off when they finally figured it out. He had known this for a long time, from before the day his Spirit set in motion, when he spoke to the chaos of the energy that was "formless and empty" saying: Let there be light' and at the command of his voice there was light! Energy at the speed of light squared (approximately 90,000,000,000 kilometers per second) became matter and the world came into existence.

After Einstein's theory, they began to realize what God was talking about through the Scriptures.

Have you ever stopped to think about the fact that there was light (Genesis 1:3) before the creation of the sun and moon (Genesis 1:14-18)? The light was Jesus. He declared himself to be the light of the world, also saying that he was with God in the beginning (John 1:1-3). Nothing was done without him. Reading the penultimate chapter of the Book of the Maker, you will see that in the New Jerusalem, Jesus, the Lamb of God, will again be the only light of the world, just as it was before the creation of the sun and the moon: The city needs neither sun nor moon to give it clarity, For the glory of God enlightens it, and the Lamb is its lamp. ' (Revelation 21:23)."

Jesus is the Messiah spoken of in the Old Scriptures, though unconverted Jews do not believe this and await the coming of the Messiah today.[222]

The fact that a man cannot remit the sins of another man required that the Messiah be the Son of God Himself.

Hence why the Messiah could be none other than the very glory of God: "Shekinah", as Aleksandr Mien wrote:[223]

> "Who can open the way to the kingdom? Who can lead the man to him?
>
> The faith of the people taught that only the Almighty can do the impossible. When he is present among the people, he purifies them and gives them spiritual strength. The rabbis called Shekinah, the invisible outpouring of the divine who comes into the world, this mystical presence of Iahweh among his people. "If two or three are united to study the law. Shekinah lives among them, "said the wise men (Avot, III, 2). This was a mystery on the threshold of which even the greatest teachers of Israel stumbled: indeed, man cannot survive the approach to God, and only the love of the Eternal, which brings down any obstacle, can unite what is irreconcilable by nature."

Jesus used to call himself the "Son of Man", referring to the fact that he assumed the physical likeness of man (= as man), as prophesied in the book of Daniel: [224]

> "I continued contemplating, when some thrones were prepared and an Elder sat down. The court took a seat and the books were opened... I kept beholding in my night visions, when I saw one like the Son of Man coming on the clouds of heaven. He stepped forward to the Elder and was introduced to his presence. To him was granted empire, honour, and kingdom, and all peoples, nations, and languages served him. Your empire is an eternal empire that will never pass and your kingdom will never be destroyed."

The prophecy about the Davidic origin of Jesus was fulfilled by the fact that Jesus was welcomed by Joseph as if he were his son, although Jesus was generated in a supernatural way. Joseph was David's direct predecessor in 28 generations and Abraham's David in 14 generations[225]

Jesus demonstrates his divine origin by quoting from Scripture:

> As the Pharisees gathered together, Jesus asked them, "What do you think about Christ? Whose son is he?"

"He is the son of David," they answered.

He said to them, "How then does David, speaking by the Spirit, call him Lord? For he says:

The Lord said to my Lord:

Sit at my right hand, until I put your enemies under your feet. '226

"If David therefore calleth him Lord,' how can he be his son?" No one could answer him a word; And from that day on, no one ever dared to ask him any questions." (Matthew 22:41 to 46, Bible of Study NIV.)

When John the Baptist was imprisoned at the behest of King Herod, he sent his disciples to Jesus to ask him, "Are you He who comes' or should we expect another?" To which Jesus replied, "Go and tell John what you have seen and heard: the blind recover their sight, the lame walk upright, the lepers are cleansed, the deaf hear, the dead rise, the good news is preached to the poor, and happy is he who does not fall because of me."[227] [228]

Jesus chose not to answer with testimony of himself, but with the facts, having invoked, once again, the Scriptures and the testimony that God the Father gave him by the working of miracles. Thus we read in Isaiah 35 (BTE):[229]

> "Let the desert and the barren land rejoice, let the steppe wax and blossom, let it be covered with flowers from the fields, let it leap and dance and shout for joy! The glory of Lebanon is given to him, the splendour of Carmel and Sharon, and the glory of the LORD will be seen, the splendour of our God. Strengthen your weary hands, make your feeble knees firm. Say to those who are troubled: Be strong, do not be afraid. This is your God: it is the vengeance that comes, the retribution of God. He himself is coming to save you. Then the eyes of the blind will see and the ears of the deaf will open. Then shall the lame man leap like a deer, and the mouth of the dumb cry for joy."

The Messiah would be born, as in fact Jesus was born in Bethlehem, as the prophet Micah had prophesied: "O Bethlehem Ephrata, you are but a little village in Judea, but it will be the place where my King, who has lived since before the world existed..." (Micah 5:2, Living Bible version). The Jewish religious leaders who were called to the presence of King Herod Antipas, the monarch of the Jews (Matthew 2:3-5), would also come to this conclusion about the place of birth.

After the birth, an angel of God appeared to Joseph and encouraged him to leave for Egypt, because King Herod intended to kill the child. That same night they departed for Egypt and remained there until the death of King Herod, fulfilling the prophecy contained in the book of Hosea 11:1: "When Israel was a little child, I loved him as my son and brought him out of Egypt". According to also to Matthew 2:15.[230]

Soon after Joseph's departure to Egypt, Herod feared that the Messiah would become a king in Judah. So he had all the boys of up to two years of age killed, and the prophecy contained in Jeremiah 31:15 was fulfilled:[231]

> "... There is a sad cry in Raman! Raquel is crying for her children. She does not want to be comforted because all her children have disappeared." (New Bible version)

> Or even, in the words of the Evangelist Matthew:

> "Cries of anguish come from Raman, Uncontained wailing; Rachel crying for her children; Inconsolable Because they are dead." (Matthew 2:18)

> Even the patriarch Jacob had already prophesied the coming of the Messiah by the

branch of Judah, when he blessed this and his descendants: [232]

"The scepter shall not depart from Judah, nor the governing staff from between his feet,

Until it comes to whom it belongs and to whom the people must obey.

He who binds his donkey to the vineyard and to the stock of his donkey's calf, he trampled his garment on the wine and his coat on the blood of grapes. "(BTE, Genesis 49:10 and 11)

We find a more specific prophecy in the book of Zechariah concerning the triumphal entry of the Messiah into Jerusalem:

"Tremble with joy, daughter of Zion!

Shout out, daughter of Jerusalem!

Behold, thy king cometh to meet thee: He is just and victorious, humble, riding a donkey - on a very young colt. It will eliminate from Ephraim the chariot of war and from Jerusalem the chariot of combat. He will break the war bow and proclaim peace to the nations. His dominion will go from sea to river and to the ends of this land." (BTE, Zechariah 9:9 to 10)

The prophecy concerning Jesus' entrance into Jerusalem was fulfilled as reported in Matthew 21:7-11 and Luke 19:30-39.

We also find other prophecies about the divine origin of the Messiah and his birth within the family that came from David:

> "Days will come - the oracle of the Lord - when I will raise up a legitimate bud to David;
>
> A king reigns with competence, defends law and justice on earth. In his time, Judah is saved, Israel dwells safely. Here is the name they will give him: "He is our righteousness, the LORD." (Bte, Jeremiah 23:5 and 6).
>
> "I will raise up a single shepherd at the head of my flock; He shall feed him: he shall be my servant David. He will feed you, be your shepherd. I the LORD will be their God, and my servant David a prince among them. I, the Lord, have spoken. I will make a covenant of peace with my flock... You are my flock, the flock of my pasture, you humans. I am your God - the oracle of the Lord GOD." (Bte, Ezekiel, 34:22 to 25 and verse 31.)

5.3 *The Giving of Christ to Death and Related Prophecies*

God sent Jesus of Nazareth to be welcomed by his people and to have an ecclesiastical reign first among the Jews, but, as he was not received by his own, by plan "b", He suffered and died of crucifixion for the sin of many, as prophesied in Isaiah 53 and by Jesus Himself:

> Matthew 20:18: "Behold, we go up to Jerusalem, and the Son of Man is delivered up to the chief priests and the scribes. They will condemn him to death. 19. And they will deliver him up to the Gentiles to be mocked, scourged, and crucified, but on the third day he will rise again."

> Matthew 17:22: "When they were gathered together in Galilee, Jesus said to them, The Son of man is about to be delivered into the hands of men; and they shall kill him; But on the third day he shall rise again. ' Then the disciples grieved greatly."

> Matthew 26:1: "When Jesus had finished all these teachings, he said to his disciples: 2. You know that in two days' time the Passover will be celebrated; And the Son of man shall be delivered up to be crucified."

> Mark 10:33: "Behold, we go up to Jerusalem, and the Son of Man is delivered up to the chief priests and scribes; They shall condemn him to death, and deliver him unto the Gentiles; And they shall mock him, and spit on him, and scourge him, and kill him; But after three days he shall rise again."

> John 13:31: "The time has come for this world
> to be judged, and now its prince will be cast out.
> And I, when I am lifted up from the earth, will
> draw all to myself."

It was Jesus himself who gave himself up for crucifixion on his way to Jerusalem as he had predicted several times, and he had the power to set himself free if he so desired. When arrested, Jesus said to the soldiers who drew their swords, "Strike your sword; For all that take the sword shall perish by the sword. Thinkest thou that I cannot pray unto my Father, and he would send me at that time more than twelve legions of angels? How then should the Scriptures be fulfilled, according to which it is to be?" (Matthew 26:52-54)

In another passage, Jesus talked, openly, about his mission and the plan of salvation:

> "The Father loves Me because I give up my life
> so that I can have my life back again. No one can
> kill Me without Me leaving; - I surrender my life
> willingly. For I have a right and the power to lay
> down my life at my will, and the right and the
> power to take it again, because the Father has
> given me that right." (John 10:17-18 - Bible in
> the "Living Bible" version.)

It is opportune to recall the severe and vehement rebuke Jesus made to Peter when he tried to dissuade him from his mission, having called Peter a "stumbling block" claiming that he was moved by the power of Satan. Let's see the passage:

> "From that time Jesus Christ began to show his disciples that he must go to Jerusalem, and suffer many things of the elders, chief priests, and scribes, and be killed, and be raised the third day.
>
> And Peter called him aside, and began to rebuke him, saying, Have mercy on thee, Lord: There's no way that's gonna happen to you.
>
> But Jesus, turning, said to Peter, Cast off! Satan; You are a stumbling block to me, because you do not think of the things of God, but of men. " (Matthew 16:21-23)

In Acts, we read that Jesus was delivered "according to the design and foreknowledge of God" and that Jesus' death was "predetermined".[233] [234]

A little dip in the political and religious atmosphere of the time gives us a very enlightening picture of the tensions surrounding the person of Jesus.

It may intrigue the fact that the main target of Jesus' criticism was the Pharisees, when it is certain that there were other political-religious factions, such as the Sadducees, the Herodians, the Essenes and the Zelotes, who had more points of disagreement with the teachings of Jesus.

David Flusser, a late scholar and former professor of comparative religion at the Hebrew University of Jerusalem, wrote:

> "Although it was not possible to detect, by means of the philological method, the escalation of tensions provoked by the evangelists, It would be difficult to understand the existence of genuine hostility towards Jesus on the part of the 'scribes and Pharisees' - a cause that allegedly contributed to his death. It is obvious that there were among the Pharisees some narrow-minded people - they are found in all societies - who suspected this miracle-worker. With satisfaction, they would have caught him in a forbidden action so they could drag him to a rabbinical court. Jesus, however, always managed to express his opinion without giving them the slightest justification to bring him to trial."

The perplexity of Flusser, however, starts from the reasoning that the teachings of Jesus most approached the Pharisee discourse to the point that the Scholar considered Christ as a "Pharisee, in a *broader* sense[235]", understanding that the "conceptions of Jesus and the Pharisees were not opposed".[236]

Flusser's argument is based on the fact that the Pharisees believed in the immortality of the soul and in the final judgment, unlike the Sadducees who did not believe in it, as they did not believe in the coming of the messiah, at least as the savior of the spirit. While the Pharisees believed in the Torah and the prophets, the Sadducees only "recognized the Pentateuch and judged secondary the writings of the prophets". The Sadducees formed a smaller group than the Pharisees, "though mighty, among the priestly aristocracy of the Temple in Jerusalem". The Herodians aligned themselves with King Herod and the Roman power, while the Zealots sought to regain power by force and awaited a warrior messiah. It was the Herodians who set a trap for Jesus, asking him, "Is it permissible to pay tribute?" Apparently, whatever the answer, it would bring disaffection and political problems to Jesus, and the answer of the Nazarene was extraordinarily wise. The Pharisees considered the Roman yoke a punishment from God, and the Zealots forbade the payment of the tribute by their adherents as commented in the letters "j" and "n" of verses 16 and 17 of Matthew 22 in the Ecumenical Bible. [237][238][239][240][241]

The Pharisees emerged in the "turbulent period of the 2nd century B.C. and opposed the dominant Maccabean dynasty, which had made alliance with the political-religious movement of the Sadducees," in the second half of the 2nd century B.C. and which usurped the priestly power of the Levites. The Pharisee term derives from the Hebrew[242] [243]"perushim" and means "the separated ones". They comprised a sect of about 6,000 members at the time of Jesus and who advocated the need to obtain purification by their isolation from public sinners and by the observance of specific rituals and other obligations that were set forth outside the Mosaic law, even under the pretext of interpreting it. [244]

Although the Pharisees, at the time of Jesus, were more concerned with religious activity, they had been merciless to their political and religious adversaries. In the time of Queen Salome Alexandra, they did not spare their Sadducee opponents. Also the manuscripts . discovered on the Dead Sea in 1947 attest that the Pharisees systematically persecuted the Essenes[245][246]

Jesus knew that the Jewish leaders, including the Pharisees, would persecute and kill the "prophets, sages, and scribes" He would send, being a hypocrite the custom of reverence for the tombs of the prophets their fathers murdered. Outraged by this, Jesus threw on that generation of Pharisees the "blood of the righteous shed upon the earth, from the blood of Abel the righteous to the blood of Zechariah the son of Barachias," slain between the "temple and the altar" (Matthew 23:35, BTE).

It seems to us that criticism of the Pharisees and scribes was directed at the fact that it was they who exercised the priesthood before the people, being responsible for their spiritual direction, but in this office they were hypocritical, because they did not practice their own discourse, although they were "sitting in the chair of Moses" (BTE). With this statement, Jesus clarified that the Pharisees had more knowledge and understanding of the law. [247] [248] [249]

Another strong criticism directed by Jesus to the Pharisees in general was that they transmitted traditions and rituals that they created outside the law that focused on highlighting secondary and less serious legal aspects, omitting the essence of it that was, in the words of Jesus, justice, mercy and fidelity. [250] [251]

The Pharisees, for example, considered gold and offerings more important than the sanctuary and the altar; taught that the oath by the altar had no consequence, while the oath by the offering required its fulfillment. Innovating the law, they imposed themselves the tithe on goods such as mint, fennel and cumin and rituals of external purification. [252][253][254][255]

Although versed in the law, many Pharisees misrepresented it, leading the people astray, which justified the strong indignation of Jesus against them, which was expressed in his zeal for the affairs of God, that is, for the House of God and for the priesthood.

The Pharisees and the scribes were the voices of the temple, charged with ministering the Word of God to the people, unlike the Sadducees and Zealots, who dealt with political and earthly affairs and the first also of the temple administration, without exerting a marked spiritual influence on the people.

All the indignation of Jesus can be condensed into the following words he issued:

> "Woe to you, coroners, who have taken the key to knowledge; You yourselves entered not, and they that would enter in, ye hindered them.[256]
>
> Woe to you, scribes and hypocritical Pharisees, you who lock the entrance of the kingdom to men! You yourselves, in fact, do not enter it, and do not let those who would like it in!
>
> Woe unto you, scribes and Pharisees, hypocrites, who travel the seas and the continents to gain one proselyte, and when you conquer it, you make it twice as worthy of Geena as you!"[257][258]

The Bible reports that Jesus' zeal for the House of God was a pretext for his crucifixion, as in the incident of the cleansing of the temple.[259]

It is precisely this zeal of God the Son for divine matters that explains his strong indignation, addressed mainly to the Pharisees in general, then responsible for the religious guidance of the people.

Notice the reader that the wrath of Jesus did not relate to the good knowledge of the Word by the Pharisees, who placed them, according to Jesus, in the "chair of Moses". Instead, Jesus recommended the people to practice what the Pharisees taught; But not what the Pharisees did. [260][261]

An important question is to understand why Jesus preferred to remain in almost total silence in the judgments preceding his death. A clear answer to this question is that it had been prophesied about him, just as the following facts were previously announced in the book of Isaiah, chapter 53: his resurrection, terrible suffering and death, the lashes, which would be counted among criminals, who would be buried among the rich, who would pray for sinners, that his death would result from an unjust and lying judgment.[262] [263] [264] [265] [266] [267] [268] [269]

Here is the biblical passage that deals with the subject: Isaiah 53 (Living Bible).

> "Who believed what we announced? To whom will the Lord reveal his power? 2. In the eyes of God he was a small branch, springing from a root on dry ground. But to us He had no beauty at all; There was nothing in Him to attract us or

to please us. 3. We despised Him and rejected Him. He was a Man who knew, from his own experience, pain and suffering. We think He did not deserve to be looked after by us; We didn't give a damn about Him.

4. In spite of this, He put upon Himself our sorrows, He Himself bore our suffering. And we kept thinking that He was being punished by God for His own sins! But this is the truth, that He was wounded for our sins: his body was mistreated because of our disobedience. He was punished for us to have peace; He was whipped - and we were healed! 6. We were lost and scattered like sheep! We forsake the ways of God and follow our own ways; Yet God has cast the guilt and sins of each one of us upon Him. 5. A

7. He was mistreated and humiliated, but did not say a single word! He was led to death as a lamb goes to the slaughter, as a sheep is silent before him who cuts his wool. He said nothing to his judges and accusers! 8. He was condemned in an unjust and lying trial; among his people no one was able to imagine why He was killed - the punishment for their sins! 9. He died as a criminal, but was buried with the rich; For he hath never done wrong, nor spoken evil of another.

10. Nevertheless, the Lord's perfect plan required his death and suffering. But after giving his life as a sin offering. He will rise again, see many children who have won through faith

<blockquote>
and successfully fulfill the will of the Lord. 11. And when He can see the result of your terrible suffering, He will be very pleased. Through all that has passed, my Servant, the Righteous One, will make many people become righteous before Me, because He Himself will take their sins upon Himself. 12. Because of this I will give Him great honors and great power, because He gave His life up to the point of going to death. He was considered a sinner; yet he took upon himself the sins of many people and prayed for God on behalf of sinners. "
</blockquote>

The suffering and death of Jesus expose our shame, our impotence and our insignificance; Finally, our sin that was shattered on the cross, while revealing the nobility, courage and the superhuman altruism of the Messiah, son of a strong, loving and wonderful God.

5.4 *Reconciliation with God through Christ*

The Messiah, who is Jesus Christ, replaced the priests of the first covenant, who were responsible for the immolation of animals from which the blood, usually of lambs, was sprinkled for the atonement of sins.

Thus Jesus was announced by John the Baptist as the "lamb that taketh away the sin of the world", and Paul exclaimed, "God made him to be sin for our sake, that we through him might become the righteousness of God" (2 Corinthians 5:21).[270]

At the Last Supper, Jesus took a cup and, "after He had given thanks, He gave it to them, saying, 'Drink from it all, for this is My blood of the Covenant, shed for the multitude, for the forgiveness of sins'" (BTE, Matthew 26:26-28).

After Jesus shed His blood, bearing upon Himself our transgressions and replacing us on the cross (remission and vicarious death), we can stand before God in the name of Jesus and be sure that we will be accepted.

Jesus not only provides us with the remission of sins, but helps us to abandon the principle that makes us sin and of which we were slaves. He is the Bread of Life.[271]

The Lord Jesus became the only High Priest who mediates between God the Father and men.[272]

Of course, having God Himself willing to send His only begotten Son into the world for the salvation of mankind, there is no other name that leads to redemption, as the only

and perfect High Priest, because the Scriptures say of Him:

> "I am the Way, the Truth and the Life. No one
> can reach the Father except through Me..."[273]

Jesus himself, associating his Person with healing and salvation, compared his raising on the tree (crucifixion) to the lifting of the bronze serpent on a stake, so that the Israelites who looked at it would not die (John 3:14).[274] [275]

The cross reveals the superhuman and extraordinary love of God for us, having Jesus emptied himself of all his kingship and power, proper to the Only-begotten Son of God the Father, to come into the world as a man, to write with his blood the most beautiful love story between a merciful God and his creation.

The plan of salvation through Jesus Christ may seem incomprehensible in human terms. The Bible reports that the cross is madness to the world. Many Jews expected that the Messiah would come in great pomp and circumstance, free the Israeli nation from the oppression of foreign peoples, and lead a secular kingdom. Humanly, one could not conceive that the

Messiah would be born in a manger, live spartanly, suffer horribly, be humiliated and die on the infamous tree for the remission of the sins of many, having been obedient to God until the end of his passage on earth. [276]

By the standards of the world, Jesus had been defeated, because the values of the world do not identify with those who are considered precious by God.

Jesus spoke openly to all using the truth, even though he knew that the truth would lead him to death. He loved first without expecting reciprocity, and even though he was infinitely greater than any human being, because he was truly the Messiah and Son of God, he placed himself at the level of the people and this was his humility.

The degree of suffering and the way Jesus died exposed the deep indignation that the good God has against sin and also the distance that separates his Holiness from sin. Berkouwer writes of this: "the distance and antithesis of sin in relation to God, in the abandonment of the Man of Sorrows (Mt 27:46), becomes definitely visible at the center of human history, and this abandonment indicates the depth of the distance between God and sin." [277]

Finally, people's lives were so impregnated with sin that the situation required a grand solution through a second great covenant with humanity.

We can only understand the offering of Jesus when we see the repulsion that the Lord God has of him. The only way to create a bridge between God and his beloved creature would be through the offering of a Lamb without blemish and without blemish, like the very Only Begotten Son of God, who has drawn the sins of mankind to himself, because no man born of woman could cancel the sin of his fellow man. sin and the wrath that sinful behavior provokes in

Jesus came to give a new nature to the redeemed, that they might worship God in spirit and in truth, no longer in feigned form. One of the most scathing criticisms of Jesus, addressed to religious leaders, was that they did not practice what they taught and when this occurred, obedience to the Mosaic law was only outward and formal, because inside they did not agree with what they practiced, or they had no sincerity toward God.

This, no doubt, also struck the ceremonial of the atonement for sins, which passed, for many, to be only an outward sign of empty religiosity devoid of sincerity and repentance.

Hence the admirable importance of the second great covenant which not only redeemed past sins, but changed the nature of the redeemed so that they might be delivered from the power that made them sin, and God would personally act upon those who repent of their sinful life, printing in their minds and in their hearts their laws (= their will). [278]

In the first covenant, the laws were engraved on the tablets of the law and God was present in the tabernacle with the intermediation of the high priest. By the second covenant, God approaches people and writes his laws directly in the mind and heart of those who accept the one High Priest, who is Jesus, the Christ.

A better understanding of this can be done by associating with the veil of the sanctuary. In the first covenant, according to Exodus 26:31, there was a veil separating the Holy place from the Most Holy. At that time, God dwelt within the veil and man outside it; this could look at the veil, but never into it. When the Lord Jesus was crucified, the veil of the Temple was torn from above to below, passing God to manifest himself directly to His people. [279]

Jesus Christ once exclaimed, "If any man thirst, let him come unto Me, and drink. Whoever believes in Me, as the Scripture says, rivers of living water will flow from within" (Bible VN).[280]

The Lord Jesus also alludes to the living water in John 4:14, adding, "But whosoever drinketh of the water that I shall give him shall never thirst for ever: On the contrary, the water I give him will be in him a fountain flowing into eternal life" (Bible VN).

When the Lord Jesus spoke in John 7:37, He made reference to the book of Numbers chapter 20, verse 13, when the Lord God directed Moses to touch the rock twice to make water flow from it to quench the people's thirst.

What is clear is that Jesus Christ is the only way to a spiritually enlivened life, the means by which God makes his presence to act in the person (not that there is an impediment to the life-giving action of God without Jesus). Jesus is the Rock. He is the stone rejected by men, who became the chief, the cornerstone, according to Matthew 21:42 and Psalm 118:22.[281] [282]

Just as by Adam's disobedience all human beings became sinners, by the obedience of Jesus Christ many may be accepted by God.[283]

Although we are born morally neutral, we are flesh and this leads us to the practice of sin, so we resemble Adam and Eve in this sense. Our character rebels against God and seeks to create human self-sufficiency and independence, which only exists in appearance.

Adam chose to disobey God and took the fruit of the tree of the knowledge of good and evil, even though he was warned of the consequence, because he understood that this fruit would give him a position of independence before God, making it possible to make his own decisions. In Watchmann

Nee's view, Adam "chose the development of his own humanity, wanting to become a better or perhaps perfect man, according to his own pattern - but separated from God. The result, however, was death, because he did not have life in himself. Divine indispensable to realize in itself the purpose of God, and ended up choosing to be an agent "independent", of the Enemy. Thus, in Adam, we all became sinners, dominated by Satan, subject to the law of sin and death and deserving the wrath of God"[284]

We received, by heredity, everything that belonged to Adam, an ephemeral life and away from God (= in sin). The choice of Adam brought us the transience of life and the carnal constitution inherited from Adam.

God's mercy and love have determined his reconciliation with man. God had a unique son who desired that many of men should become his Sons by adoption and be co-participants in the divine family, being spiritually quickened.[285]

The purpose of God, to make His only begotten Son (Jesus) the Firstborn Son, was fulfilled in the manner explained by Jesus: "Verily, verily, I say unto you, Except a grain of wheat fall into the earth and die it shall remain alone; but if he dies he will bear much fruit".[286]

This only grain of wheat that God had, his own only begotten Son, was delivered up to be killed, having, in his resurrection, drawn many to himself, who, through faith, received the grace to be delivered from sin and death, becoming God's children.

At the end of John's gospel, Jesus says to Mary Magdalene, "... but go to my brethren, and say unto them, I ascend unto my Father and your Father: to my God and your God." Affectionately, the Lord Jesus calls his disciples brothers. Until then, when referring to Yahweh, he usually used the possessive pronoun in the first person ("my Father").[287]

It is that Jesus transmits to the redeemed a new nature that accredits them to become Sons of God, no longer just creatures. The Beloved Disciple taught that: "But to those who received him, to those who believe in his name, he gave the power to become children of God. These were not born of blood, nor of the will of the flesh, nor of the will of man, but of God" (Bte, John 1:12-13).

How is deliverance from sin? Through the conviction (faith) that we are in Christ and our fleshly and sinful nature was crucified with Christ and that we were welcomed as Sons of God.

To assume divine sonship, there is need of a new life, which is not an independent or liberated life; she is a life bound to Christ.

While we live in sin, the Bible says that we are in disgrace, living as dead to God and under the dominion of carnal passions and selfishness, in short, of sin.

The converted person dies to sin and begins to have a spiritual life linked to Jesus. He becomes averse to things he once enjoyed (sins) and begins to like other things very much, which he once despised and even hated (Christian practices). It is God Himself acting in the life of the person showing him what is pleasing to him or not. God, however, does not interfere in the individuality of the person, only removes what is unclean in him, modifying the heart and mind. The mind is modified because God helps us to abandon impure thoughts and fills our soul with noble and positive ideas. Negative feelings, such as hurt feelings, sadness, guilt, anger, hatred, are replaced by noble feelings such as kindness, love, trust, and self-esteem. Many people are transformed and give up addictions from which they were held for many years, such as promiscuity, drugs, drinks and cigarettes.[288]

Thus, by Adam's disobedience, all human beings became sinners, by obedience to Jesus Christ many may be justified.

6   The reconciliation with God. The steps of the Way

6.1   Go to meet God

Mere indifference to the things of God reveals a sinful attitude which results in turning away from him.

It is not enough to be interested in the subject, God seeks people who dedicate fidelity to it, worshipping it in spirit and in truth.[289]

It is no wonder that the Lord Jesus cited fidelity as one of the important aspects of the divine commandments, alongside justice and mercy.[290]

While righteousness relates to our behavior toward others, faithfulness is linked to direct relationship with the Lord God. Faithfulness therefore speaks more closely with the first four commandments of Exodus 20 and with the first great commandment uttered by Jesus.

It is important to approach in fear of God.

God is pleased when we fear Him and recognize His infinite greatness and sovereignty. He was pleased with

Abraham and considered him to be tried, because of the fear that he devoted to the Most High as read in the following Biblical passage:

> "And when they came to the place which God had appointed him, Abraham set up an altar there, and set the logs of wood. He tied his son Isaac up and put him on the wood. Abraham reached out to grab the cleaver and kill his son. Then the angel of the LORD called out from heaven and exclaimed, "Abraham! Abraham!" He replied, "Here I am." He continued, Do not stretch out your hand against the young man. Do nothing to him, for now **I know that you fear God, you who have not spared your son, your only son, for me."** (BTE, Genesis 22:9-13)

The fear of God is also linked to the fulfillment of the first commandment: "I am the LORD your God... you shall have no other gods before me."

To our parents we must pay special respect. We tend to revere special treatments, important people and authorities.

To Yahweh we owe much more than that, we must yield to him - and to Him alone - worship! Worship is to render worship and praise to the Most High, recognizing him as

Almighty Creator, upon whom we are dependent. of all things and only God, All

No one is outside divine authority: we are all subject to the sovereignty of God and we may be accountable for what we do of our intellectual autonomy, except those who pass from death to life. God the Son was very emphatic in his parables about the responsibility of each one before God. [291][292][293]

We often read in the Bible that the fear of God is a predicate much appreciated by God and that it has always accompanied the great biblical figures, such as Abraham, Jacob, Joseph and Job. [294][295][296][297]

God's sovereignty in no way means that He is far from us. So much so that he sent us his Only Son so that all people would have the opportunity to live eternally with him.

God always answers our prayers, but we don't always get the answer we want. It can be "yes", "no", "wait", or "I have something better for you".

My personal experience has taught me that we must insist on knocking. As an adult, I heard my mother tell of her experience with the Holy Spirit in wonder. I longed to have that experience, but I thought it was not for me, or that I was not worthy or entitled to receive it.

But I didn't give up, I memorized Bible verses and I tried to have a straight life before God. Until the age of 32, I had my experience with the Holy Spirit, being flooded by it.

That was the most remarkable experience of my life! I could feel God's care and love for me.

Another step to commune with God is to always be in his presence with faith, because:

> "... without faith it is impossible to please God, for he who comes to God must believe that he exists and reward those who seek him." (Hebrews 11:6, Ecumenical Bible version.)

To believe is to be convinced of spiritual reality, which is beyond human perception.

Today, we live in the so-called information age. The computer revolutionized the capacity of data storage and human communication.

At school we learn that man is descended from the ape, or from a hominid, and that planet Earth arose from a large accidental explosion.

Almost no space is opened in schools or universities for theories, also scientific, that oppose evolutionism and work with the hypothesis of the creation of the Earth by a Superior Being (creationists), defending the harmonious coexistence between religion and science.

Creationists argue that the so-called "big-bang" - possible great explosion that originated the universe -might well be co-ordinated totally by God, strong in the argument that life could not arise from an accidental explosion, by the mathematical and physical impossibility of everything being so perfectly and intricately grouped as it is today.

This constitutes a barrier to the acceptance of the faith in our day, especially by the youth. At arm wrestling, atheist scientists practically banned religious education in Brazilian schools, leaving students obliged to hear only one of the scientific theses (yes, because creationism is also a scientific thesis!).

The Bible speaks of the importance of parents teaching their children the ways of God from an early age. It is very difficult for parents to teach the Bible at home while the teacher transmits a godless existence.

It is unfortunate that the atmosphere of disbelief is being formed in schools, where the theory of the evolution of man is transmitted down the throat of adolescents as if it were a fait accompli. In fact, evolution is a scientific theory, as much as creationism is.

The arguments and evidences of creationist theory are simply ignored, although human science cannot explain the so-called "lost links" of the theory of evolution; nor the logical impossibility of everything being perfectly ordered from a spontaneous and casual explosion; the deficiencies and inaccuracies of carbon 14 dating over time. [298]

Schools should present both theories through a scientific approach, and not impose upon students the acceptance of evolutionary theory as if it were an undisputed truth.

Wernher Von Braun, in introducing the work "Darwin and his Macadam", by Harold Hill, wrote: [299]

> "To me, the idea of creation is inconceivable without God. No one can stand before law and order in the universe without concluding that there must be, after all, a divine purpose.
>
> Some evolutionists believe that creation is the result of the casual arrangement of atoms and molecules over billions of years. However, when they consider the development of the human brain by the casual process of a short period of time less than a million years, they are obliged to admit that such a period of time is not exactly sufficient. Or, take the evolution of the eye in the animal world. What casual process could possibly explain the simultaneous evolution of the optical system that governs the world of vision, the nerve filaments that conduct the optical signals from the eye to the brain and the central optic nerve in the brain, where the luminous impulses are converted into images, that the conscious mind can understand.

The Word of God cannot be fully addressed, studied or investigated by scientific means known to man, by the limitation of his methods and instruments.

The spiritual world is above the possibility of man's intellect. God blessed Man and determined that all creation submit to Him (Genesis 1:28-30); However, God did not confer upon Him the complete intellectual understanding of the spiritual world.

A friend of mine exclaimed, as we watched a television report about transgenics: "This I know you can do; I doubt, however, that man can create life".[300]

In fact, man can prepare the environment and the favorable conditions for life to develop, but he cannot create it.

Indeed, human science is incapable of manufacturing a seed in the laboratory. Therefore, by scientific methods, it cannot explain life itself. Science does not fully explain the formation of life, and yet it does not cease to exist.

The unbeliever resembles the man described by Plato who always lived inside a cave, in chains, where he only saw shadows and assumed that this was the reality.

We must leave the cave, be guided by the eyes of faith and marvel at the real presence of God! When we take this step of faith, we will experience what science cannot explain.

Whoever tries to explain the Bible from human science, is limiting God to known human parameters and rejects the greatest gift God gives to all people, which is faith:

> "In the name of the grace that is given to me, I say to each one of you: Do not pretend beyond reason, be reasonable enough not to be pretentious, each according to the measure of faith with which God has given him." (Romans 12:3 - Bible Ecumenical Translation)

Jesus also confirmed that faith proceeds from God when, in telling the parable of the sower, he compares the word of God to the seed (Mark 4:1-9; Matthew 13:1-9).

God is extremely merciful and kind when He established the criterion of faith to accept us into His kingdom at the expense of the strict and absolute application of justice, because the Bible teaches that there is not even one righteous person, for all, one by one, have gone astray.

Justifying faith has a well-defined and delineated object. Although "believe" constitutes an intransitive verb according to Portuguese grammar, the phrase is only complete with a complement to its perfect understanding. We need to know what's right, what's right in who's right for what's right.

It is not enough to believe in God as a Higher Being and to think that all religions are good. This statement is only true in the sense that all religions, in a general way, co-operate for the advancement and develop principles of morality for man. But the Bible clearly speaks that there is only one way to quicken the soul and salvation without judgment. The regenerates will be saved by this general rule, but many others will be saved through divine judgment, which I will deal with in my work "God's conditional love (in)".

Faith, of which God is pleased, is faith in his word. The Bible is our "manual of the maker". When we have any doubts about a product we purchase, we use the manufacturer's manual. Likewise, when we need guidance from our Creator regarding our lives, we must follow the prescriptions he has bequeathed to us for the solution of our everyday problems. He knows us better than any doctor. He gave us life!

Many people believe the broad outlines of the Bible, failing to believe certain biblical accounts, arguing that it was written by men, who may have failed in their mission. Many still prefer to constitute their "private Bible", pinching certain passages that interest them and despising others that are not convenient for them.

This is a confession of unbelief in the Almighty God. The "god" of these people is not the God of the Bible, since for Him nothing is impossible.

If we believe that God is Almighty, then we cannot doubt that He has left us His true Word. And He is exceedingly zealous for His Word.

The unbeliever does not approach God, because faith corresponds to the part (minimum) that is ours to enjoy His presence. The Lord God has already done the difficult - and humanly impossible - part of sending to the world his only begotten Son, the lamb without blemish, so that, suffering and dying in a terrible way, he would provide us with the real chance of salvation, since, if God judged the world by severe justice (= individual merits), few would be saved. Therefore, if you do not do the minimum part that befits you, God will not be able to approach you and turn the amorphous clay into a vessel of blessings.[301]

It is essential to read the Bible with credulity, because God proclaims that:

> "the word that proceedeth out of my mouth: it bringeth it not to me without fruit; but it executeth my will, and secureth the success of the mission for which I sent it."[302]

If we believe in the Bible, we know that it all leads to Jesus, who is the Messiah himself and the only High Priest, through whom we can obtain, by faith, the forgiveness of sins and salvation. No other name is accredited by God to function as our intercessor and Advocate. It is that God the Father, in remembrance of the sacrifice of his only begotten Son, has appeased his wrath and can take away our guilt, because Jesus' sacrifice is able to redeem us from the death produced by sin.[303]

Jesus Christ, the Sent Son of God, took upon himself all our transgressions, replacing the suffering and death that the chosen ones deserve to go through because of their sins.

To go to meet God, you need to know to whom you must address yourself: to God the Father in the name of His Son.

Jesus Christ, because he is the Way, the Truth and the Life, no one goes to the Father except through him[304]

We must invoke Jesus Christ as the only High Priest, since his Name is above any name, and there is no other teaching that brings redemption and reconciliation with God. [305]

It is important to stress that the name of Jesus, the Christ, has no magical property, because those who seek magical power in things, such as blood, cross or images, are being idolatrous and occult. Magic and incantations are Satan's means of action.

When we make a request "in the name of Jesus" we are recognizing that He is truly the Messiah, the only intercessor between God and men.

Although Jesus is the foundation of faith, that is, the most basic and rudimentary in Christianity, many people, including those who consider themselves Christian, insist on distorting this essential truth.

Many believe that dead people can perform miracles or intercede for them before God. It's not just demigods. A small Brazilian city was literally "disappearing" from the map, until a priest had the idea of starting a religious tourism to worship a supposed saint. The city began to receive pilgrimages from all over the country, who rushed to worship the saint. Nothing against the development of the city and the recognition of the value of a person dedicated to religion. However, I see that the provision of worship to saints, or the belief in their intercession, has no biblical support and can divert many people from the true path.It is abominable to invoke dead people, as it is also wrong to worship them as if they were dead.

It does not help us to have a belief in a Higher Being if we do not accept the One who can lead us to God, and that One is Jesus, the only begotten son of God.

Dispose of any type of image, sculpture, photographs, etc. that may lead you or anyone else to worship images, people, or false gods, or to admit any other intercessor between God the Father and men, other than the Risen Christ.

Jesus is the cornerstone of the building of the Temple of God. It is essential to recognize the divine nature of the Risen Christ as a partaker of the Heavenly Council, and all honors and worship are due to Jehovah. Jesus is not an "evolved spirit" as some proclaim without contrary to the Scriptures, but the only begotten Son of God.[306][307][308]

The fact that Jesus said that sin against him could be forgiven does not mean that he admits it by the mouth of one who has knowledge of the truth, or who has already experienced the new life. Nor should it be forgotten that the Risen Christ will, in the final judgment, reject those who deny him and those who are ashamed of him.[309]

Occultism, in all its forms, has attracted many people by the power and mystique that surround it. But if anyone wishes to become entangled in the occult, make no mistake that he is seeking God, because salvation and the Christian life are not outside of the Holy Scriptures, nor in mystical and mysterious teachings.

Jesus came to clarify the things that had hitherto been covered up and to externalize God's plan for the salvation of mankind, which was prophesied in the Scriptures.

As we have seen in the Scriptures:

> "... Jesus exulted under the action of the Holy Spirit and said, I praise you, Father, Lord of heaven and earth, for having hidden this from the wise and the intelligent, and for having

revealed it to little ones. Yes, Father, this is how you have disposed in your benevolence. "(Bte, Luke 10:21)

This exclamation of Jesus occurred on the occasion of the joyful return of the seventy-two disciples who were commissioned to announce the coming of the Kingdom of God and who experienced the power of God.

The Word of God is accessible to all, especially to the little ones who have easily understood the simple and direct language of Jesus and recognize divine intercession in miracles. The Word is hidden from the wise men of this world, because they refuse to accept the Gospel.

All that is shrouded in mysticism does not proceed from God. The symbols and rituals of occultism lead to the cult of the creature and satanic and make an apology for worldly power, but never lead to rapprochement with God.

Those who rely on horoscopes, healers, or the Cabala in the vain search for the solution of their problems and difficulties, have no faith in Jesus. When we have Jesus, we know that He cares for us as the Good Shepherd; Take care of each of your sheep and call them by name! We need not fear, even when we walk through the valley of the shadow of death, because the Good Shepherd is feeding his sheep all the time. If we allow doubt to invade our mind and heart, we no longer have faith and God cannot act in our lives. Therefore, it is essential that we abandon every kind of magic, horoscope, fortune reading, etc. and entrust our lives entirely to following in the footsteps of Jesus. [310] [311]

Because the redeemed have received from Jesus a new nature and enjoy the freedom to move within the luminous and pleasant space where God is, freely doing whatever they desire, that is, everything that spontaneously guides and requires the new nature in Christ, being no longer under the influence of the power that made them sin and considering sin repugnant.

God appreciates the insistence of his children. Therefore, do not give up before the first difficulties that will precede your goals and address your prayers to God with insistence. The Lord Jesus left us the Parable of the Importunate Friend, small in length, but immense in teaching.

Who among us would fail to answer to a friend who knocks at our door - in the middle of the night - to ask for three loaves of bread that he needs to serve unexpected visitors? The Lord Jesus reminds us that, in this situation, any one of us would open the doors of the house that were already locked and provide everything that the friend needed, if not by friendship, at least by the insistence of the friend. [312]

Who's the friend of the house? It's the Lord God. We can be the importunate friend, or the persevering friend, who, thanks to his insistence, can be received and attended by God. Jesus teaches us that:

> "Ask and it will be given to you; seek and ye shall find; Knock and it will be opened. For everyone who asks receives; what you seek, you find; And to him that knocks, it will open. Which of you, being a father, if the son shall ask of him a fish, shall he give him a serpent instead of a fish? Or if he asks for an egg, will he give him a scorpion? If you then, who are evil, know how to give good gifts to your children, how much more will the Father in heaven give the Holy Spirit to those who ask him!" (Luke 11:9 to 13)

The Lord Jesus is at the door and knocks, but many refuse the invitation. The Lord Jesus told a parable of a man who gave a great dinner and invited many. However, one by one, all the guests were giving a pretext not to attend the party. And the man commanded his servant to go into the streets and streets of the city, and to bring in the poor, and the crippled, and the blind, and the lame. When this was done and there was still room, the man commanded the servant to go through the paths and paths and force the people to enter until the house was full. The Lord Jesus concluded the parable by saying that "none of those who have been invited will taste my dinner".[313] [314]

The parable is not referring to any festivity. The feast may represent both the joy of the saved in heaven and the joy of abundant life here on earth. But apparent and false security that the world offers, or because they are accommodated in their comfortable positions, sometimes even in the pews of churches. many are despising the call of God, because they prefer to have the

The daily search for God becomes a necessity and an incomparable pleasure for all those who love and seek Him. Jesus is the Bread of Life that satisfies our hunger for God's daily presence in our lives:

"I am the living bread that comes down from heaven. Whoever eats this bread will live for eternity. And the bread that I will give is my flesh, given that the world may have life. Hearing this, the Jews began to quarrel violently among themselves: How can this man give us his flesh to eat? 'Then said Jesus unto them, Verily, verily, I say unto you, Except ye eat the flesh of the Son of man, and drink his blood, ye shall not have the life that eateth my flesh, and drinketh my blood, have everlasting life, and I will raise it up at the last day. For my flesh is true food and my blood is true drink. He that eateth my flesh, and drinketh my blood, dwelleth in me, and I in him. And as the living Father hath sent me, and I live by the Father, so he that eateth of me shall live by me. This is the bread which came down from heaven: it is very different from that which your fathers ate: For they died, but he that eateth of this bread shall live unto eternity." (John 5:48-59)

To seek God means to walk freely to where our nature in Christ takes us. The redeemed are under the law of love and freedom. The redeemed who violence his new nature in Christ and comes out of the luminous and loving company of God and seeks the darkness of sin, turns away from God.

Seeking God also means framing your life within the context of the Word of God, having a daily relationship with Jesus through prayer, reading the Bible, communion with your brothers and sisters, so that we may live within the freedom offered by the new nature in Christ, For the redeemed spontaneously do what they want to do, and therein lies their freedom: to have a pleasing life before God.

Remember everyone who comes to the Lord Jesus will in no way be cast out; shall never be left by Him; will never be abandoned (Deuteronomy 31:6).

6.2 *Sincerely repenting*

For God to act fully in a person's life, he must acknowledge his sins and sincerely repent of them.

Jesus cannot be our Advocate if we consider the sinful life to be good and glamorous and if we are proud of the sinful acts we practice. We also have no reward from God if we are lukewarm Christians (Revelation 3:16), keeping appearances and committing "hidden" sins.

The conscience of the person who is entangled in sin becomes insensitive.

Another terrible habit is to seek pretexts for our sins without actually wanting to give them up.

I ask because I am against the law of God and I continue in this attitude of rebellion when, instead of repenting and confessing my faults, I try to defend my wrong attitudes before God, harming myself.

This is called recalcitring against the pricks, an expression that the Lord God used to rebuke Saul on the way to Damascus: "Saul, Saul, why are you persecuting me? Hard thing is to recalcitrate against the goads" (ALMEIDA, Acts 26:14).

The goads were iron tips placed in the plows to teach the young oxen not to curb the plows. When we resist God, even knowing the new life in Christ, we are recalcitring against the pricks, that is, resisting aimlessly and to our detriment.

The First Couple tried to find excuses to be absolved of their sin against God. Adam blamed Eve, saying that she gave him the fruit and Eve, in turn, blamed the serpent, who seduced her. Often, we have this attitude toward God and we don't recognize our mistakes, we just try to give some explanation that can satisfy our conscience.

Berkouwer writes on this subject: [315]

> "It must be said that the most evident sign of true confession is the attitude of not agreeing with the relations of sin and the tendency to excuse oneself by denying one's own guilt (Prov. 30:20). Only when guilt is not hidden, but confessed, does the Lord become a shelter in need; when life is preserved from tribulation and surrounded by joyful songs of deliverance, in spite of all guilt." (Ps. 32:7)

God is pleased with a truly contrite heart. Jesus illustrated God's compassion for the prayers of two Israelites who were in the temple. One of the Israelites assumed an attitude of presumptuous superiority, praising his weekly fasting practice and his effort to observe the law, which distinguished him from the tax collector, who was also in the temple and whom he despised. Meanwhile, the tax collector beat his chest and cried "O God, have compassion on the sinner that I am".

Jesus with this lesson made it clear that God pitied the tax collector, whose sincere repentance gave opportunity to God's redemptive action, who returned to his justified home, while the Pharisee's prayer was not accepted by God, by virtue of his presumption and pride.[316]

The word mercy is formed by two radical groups: "miser" (wretched, miserable, *unhappy, poor person) and "cor/Cordis" (heart, **compassion**) and means to have compassion with the wretched.*

God has compassion on those who suffer because of sin and their departure from Him, as His Word tells us, even in the time of Moses:

> "But they will confess their fault and that of their fathers, saying that they have committed a sacrilege toward me, that they have even opposed me, that then I opposed them and led them into the land of their enemies; Or else, one day, their uncircumcised heart will humble itself and their punishment will be fulfilled."[317]

If you are not satisfied with a life without God and if you do not conform to the pleasures the world provides and seek happiness from on high, you must seek God's mercy and forgiveness, taking an attitude of sincere repentance, as David did in Psalm 51:

> "Have mercy on me, my God, according to your faithfulness; according to your great mercy, erase my guilt. Wash me completely from my iniquity, and cleanse me from my sin. For I acknowledge my guilt, continually bearing in

mind my sin. I have sinned against thee, and
only against thee have I done that which is evil
in thy sight: so you'll be fair when you speak,
blameless when you judge.

I was begotten in iniquity, and conceived in sin
of my mother's burning. You love the truth in
the darkness, in my night, you make me know
the wisdom. Take away my sin with hyssop, and
I will be pure; wash me and I will be whiter than
snow." (BTE, verses 9) 1 a

No matter how far you are from God and involved in a life of sin, the Bible teaches that "if your sins are like scarlet, you will become white as snow. If they are red like crimson, they shall become like wool" (Isaiah 1:18, version BTP).

When the Pharisees criticized Jesus for being at the table with tax collectors and "sinners," He argued, "It is not those who have health who need a doctor, but the sick. Go therefore and learn what it means: It is mercy that I desire, not sacrifice. For I have come to call not the righteous, but sinners" (Matthew 9:12 and 13, in the Ecumenical Bible Translation).

The patient needs to recognise his sick state, because otherwise he will not even look for a doctor and, even if he comes looking for him, he will not follow the treatment that he prescribed.

As long as you consider yourself good, just and self-sufficient and find a thousand and one pretext to justify your sinful life, God will not fully operate in your life. When we take on the position of sinners, God's wonders will begin to happen in our lives.

Even Job, who was considered the wisest man of the Orientals, "upright and upright, who feared God and kept himself away from evil", had to be broken by God to understand the divine sovereignty, the smallness of man and the foolishness of human wisdom. [318]

At the height of his suffering, he continues to defend his integrity, but comes to criticize a supposed absence of God (23:1-9) and attacks the injustice of society, as if to complain of an alleged and incomplete divine interference on the earthly plane.[319]

The LORD God Himself comes to assert His sovereignty over all things in chapters 38 and 39, challenging Job as follows:

> "Who is denigrating providence with meaningless speeches?
>
> Gird up your kidneys like a mighty man; I will question you, and you will instruct me.

Where were you when I founded the earth?

Tell me this, you wise man.

Do you know who measured it?

Who laid the string on her?

Into what are its pillars, the cornerstone, the one who cast it, to the choral singing of the morning stars and to the acclamation of the Sons of God?" (Job 38: 7, Bible version Ecumenical Translation.) 1 a

At the beginning of Chapter 40, God challenges Job: "Does the contender of the Mighty still criticize? Answer, therefore, what reproaches God!" Job answers him this way: "I am insignificant, what shall I answer? I put my hand over my mouth. I have spoken once, I say nothing more; Twice... I will add nothing".[320]

After that, the LORD God resumes the second challenge to Job, highlighting the contingent position of self and his right to judge humanity: man in relation to

"Gird up thy kidneys like a mighty man. I will interrogate you and you will instruct me. Do you really intend to dismiss my trial, convict me to justify you?

Have you an arm like God, Your voice thunders like his? Adorn thyself with majesty and greatness, clothe thyself with glory and splendor.

Give free rein to the waves of your wrath, humiliate the proud with a look.

Bend with your eyes all the proud, crush the wicked in place.

All together, mix them in the dust, gag them forever in the dungeon. So I will praise you, for your right hand has won you victory." (Chapter 40:7 to 14, Bible version)

Finally, in Chapter 42, we read Job's portrayal of the Lord God:

"'I know that you can do everything, that no project escapes your power. Who is denigrating providence without cause"? Yes, I approached, without knowing it, wonders beyond me, who did not understand. I Listen to me', I said, since the word is with you' will I interrogate you and you will instruct me?

Just hearing you say I knew you; But now you've seen my eyes.

Also, therefore, I abhor myself and portray myself in dust and ashes." (verses 6 of the same biblical version.) 1 a

Well on the subject of repentance, we can quote the man who was crucified next to Jesus, was saved and accompanied the Son God to paradise by virtue of his fear of God and sincere repentance:

> "One of the evildoers crucified insulted him: Are you not the Messiah? Save thyself, and us also!" But the other rebuked him, saying, Thou hast not the fear of God, thou that art so grieved! It is right for us to receive what our deeds have deserved; But he did nothing wrong. He said: Jesus, remember me when you come as king'. Jesus answered, Verily I say unto thee, This day thou shalt be with me in paradise. '" (BTE, Luke 23:39 to 43).

How wonderful! A contrite heart opens the gates of heaven.

The Lord Jesus suffered humiliations, received whips and lashes, died in one of the most horrible and painful ways possible, all out of love for the human being. The Blood of Christ has already been accepted by God the Father as an effective atonement for the sins of all who receive it. .

It lacks his decision to converge his will with the will of God, accepting the plan of salvation and declaring the Lord Jesus as the teacher and savior of his life, repenting from his sinful life. You can accept Jesus at this time. God can change your life no matter what your problems. Jesus invites him: "Come unto me them that labour under the burden of their burden, and I will give rest. Take my yoke upon you and learn from me, for I am meek and humble of heart, and you will find rest for your souls, for my yoke is easy my burden is light".[321]

For this, you can say a simple prayer, acknowledging your sins and asking God to forgive you, that is, remove the blame. Don't worry if you haven't felt any different emotions. If your conscience has been reached and you have felt convinced of sin, it is clear demonstration that God is at work in your life. Paul teaches that "no one can say the Lord Jesus! But by the Holy Spirit" (1st Epistle to the Corinthians 12:3, final part). Accepting divine truths by faith, we should not consult our emotional state.

After conversion, if we sin occasionally, we can appear before God and ask forgiveness in the name of Jesus Christ, because "if we confess our sins, he is faithful and just: to forgive our sins and to cleanse us from all unrighteousness".[322]

The word "repentance" comes from the Greek "metanoia", *which* means change of mind. According to John L. Mackenzie's "Biblical Dictionary", it means "change of mind' or change of heart', that is, change of intention, of disposition, of attitudes; weigh; conversion; pain because of sin. [323]

After conversion, the believer will no longer live immersed in sin, which will arise only as an accident in his life.

6.3 *Living by faith*

The faith that brings us closer to God invites us to always ask: what is the will of God in this situation?

Faith comes through preaching, and through it we know God's will for our lives.

In order for the Word to produce results for our benefit, we must be receptive to the Word and ready to abide by God's guidance.

When the redeemed is receptive to the Word, it means that he is acting according to his new nature and is placing himself under the shepherding of Jesus.

It is not enough just to wish Jesus to grant us salvation, we must submit our lives to his leadership. Jesus only shepherds the sheep who know him and hear his voice.

We can understand the nature of justifying faith when we analyze the episode related to Adamic sin.

At first, the First Couple depended exclusively on God, from whom they received everything they needed to survive. You didn't have to work hard or worry about the next day. His activity was to do the will of God at that time, which consisted in administering the rest of creation on earth, communing with God at the end of the day.

With the fall of Man, the focus of his attention shifted. He was no longer with the things of God; Now Adam and Eve were destitute of the fellowship and glory of God, and their occupation from then on centered on themselves; finally in their earthly survival, since that was all they had left.

Well, the possibility of mankind depending on God and communing with Him was re-established by God the Son. The veil of the Sanctuary has been torn in two and now we have a real opportunity, which is within the reach of anyone, to receive God's presence through Christ.

God's purpose for our lives is to accept Jesus as our teacher and savior.

We can clearly understand the function of faith in Christ, we must understand the value of Jesus' offering to God and to ourselves.

The blood shed by Jesus has the power to remit the sins of those who sincerely repent. [324]

God, however, was not content to just redeem past sins, propitiating us to a new life through Jesus, so that we might abandon the bondage of sin because of the new nature we have received from Christ. Jesus is the bread of life. [325]

The apostle Paul liked to emphasize death to sin by associating it with the cross. He said that the believer was crucified with Christ, finding himself dead to sin. [326]

In this regard, Watchman Nee wrote, in "The Normal Christian Life", sin offers a twofold problematic aspect. If we read carefully the first eight chapters of Romans, we find that there is a logical subdivision of matter, the first, corresponding to the first four and a half chapters (5.11) deals with sins [327]1.1 a*in the* plural, while the second half, composed of the remaining three and a half chapters (5:12 to 8:39) care for sin in the singular. Why does this occur? asks the Writer. Your answer comes next:

"For in the first section we consider the matter of the sins which I have committed before God, which are many, and which may be enumerated, whereas in the second, it concerns sin as the working principle of what sins I commit, It is always the principle of sin that leads me to commit them. I need forgiveness for my sins, but I also need to be delivered from the power of sin. The first touch my conscience, the last my life. I can receive forgiveness for all my sins, but because of my sin I still have no permanent inner peace. em mim. Sejam

When the Light of God shines, for the first time, in my heart, I cry for forgiveness, because I understand that I have committed sins before Him; But after I have received the forgiveness of sins, I make a new discovery, that is, the discovery of sin, and understand that I have not only committed sins before God, but also that there is something wrong within me. I find I have the nature of a sinner. There is within me an inclination to sin, an inner power that leads to sin. When that power is loose, I commit sins. I can seek and receive forgiveness, but then again. And so life continues in a vicious circle of sinning and being forgiven and then sinning again. I appreciate the blessed fact of God's forgiveness, but I desire something more than that: I need deliverance. I need forgiveness for what I've done, but I also need to be released from what I am.

How can we be sure that our sins have been forgiven. Through faith, for the Scriptures say, "If we confess our sins, he is faithful and just to forgive us, and to cleanse us from all iniquity."

There is always a consistent faith that moves the work of the Christian. It is faith that triggers all the divine help and guidance that the Christian has in his life.

But what is faith? According to Hebrews 11:1 "it is the assurance of things hoped for and the conviction of things not seen".

Faith is the certainty of facts we do not witness and hope is the conviction of facts to come.

The faith that justifies us (Romans 3:21-31; 5:1) is a specific faith, the acceptance that the blood shed by Jesus enables the sins of those who have received it to be remitted, and more, that the death of Jesus on the cross also frees us from the power that sin had over us, the redeemed. [328][329][330]

The last words of the Lord Jesus, before His death from the cross, were: "It is **finished.**"[331]

This means that the suffering and death suffered by the Lord Jesus - and painful death on the cross - was the sufficient and accepted offering by God to remit the sins of the people who receive Jesus. We can say that, symbolically, the blood deals with past sins and the cross acts on the sinful nature, because we were crucified with Christ when we received the new nature of Christ. [332]

It is important that you accept that the work of Christ is finished with the death of Him on the tree, it being utterly misplaced that you offer new offerings or penance with a view to the atonement for sins already confessed, because the remission of sins has already been made available to you at the time of the death of the cross. Those who receive Jesus as their master of their lives may consider that their old sinful nature has been crucified and extinguished by giving way to a new man/woman who walks in newness of life.

This transformation is explained by Paul in Romans 6:

> "1. What shall we say then? That we must remain in sin in order that grace may reach its fullness? 2. By no means! We who die to sin, how should we still live in it? 3. Or do you not know that all of us who have been baptized, are we baptized in his death? For by baptism we were buried with him in death so that, as Christ was raised from the dead by the glory of the Father, so we also live new life." em Cristo Jesus

These facts must be accepted by faith, for neither I nor you have been to Golgotha to witness the facts that the story relates. We could doubt these facts as we doubt so many other historical facts, much more recent, that the newspapers report daily.

Thus, it would be totally in vain for anyone to die hoping that it could cleanse him from sin, since Jesus has already taken upon Himself all our past transgressions and removed us from bondage to sin, His offering was perfect and consummated. It is we who should suffer on the cross and deserve death, but God, in his mercy, has replaced us on the cross with his beloved Son, so that we may be accepted and welcomed as children.

Only the cross of Jesus was the complete and acceptable offering before God the Father, because only Jesus had no sin and could be the spotless lamb that takes away the sin of the world.

Jesus taught that if we do not become like children, we will not enter the kingdom of heaven (Bte, Matthew 18:3).

This Jesus said because we need to have the faith that a child puts in his father. When we accept Jesus, we accept the sonship that God offers us. I like to associate faith with a weaned child: she simply stops crying when her mother takes her in her arms. But why does this happen? After all none of their needs have been met, which can be hunger or discomfort. This is because the child has faith that his mother, before this is provided, will supply all his needs. The mother even knows the child's cry, whether it is a cry of hunger or not.

Thus, too, we are to deliver ourselves into the hands of the Father, "as a child borne of a mother" (BTE, Psalm 131:2).

It is easy to think of God and to seek faith in difficult moments in life, such as when an accident occurs, or when a loved one dies. It is also easy to reflect on God on the day he goes to church. In the rest of the time, it is common for people to be so busy with their routine chores and problems that they forget to seek communion with God.

What is the space that we are reserving for God in our lives, in our hearts and in our minds? Is God just a "last resort" that we use in case of need, such as unemployment, illness, etc.? Do we only remember God in moments of extreme joy or difficulty? So we have the same consideration for God that we have for our bank manager. Just a superficial and formal relationship, cultivated for a moment of need.

Accepting Jesus is not buying a stamped ticket that we keep in our wallet to be used only at the end of time. Accepting Jesus is the beginning of a journey.

Are we doing God's will if we make communion with him a special and daily occasion of joy and sharing problems, of praise and adoration, of confession and intercession? Do we really seek God with all our heart and all our minds? Remember the first great commandment of Master Jesus: To love God with all your mind, with all your soul; above all things.

How much sin are we willing to deprive ourselves of in our life? A few, many, or all? Whether unconsciously or not we are reserving some "little sins," often hidden sins, something goes very wrong in our relationship with God. If we graduate the intensity of sin into serious and light, first. we may also be mistaken, because we may conclude that some of them could be carried out deliberately, which would be a great mistake as we have already dealt with in Chapter

God is pleased with the contrite heart and obedience of those who render him worship. As taught the Master Jesus: when we point the speck in the eye of a determined brother, we may be failing to see the stick that is covering our eyes, and we will be judged to the same extent as we use to judge others.[333][334]

Walking with the Saviour gives us abundant life. He tells us, "I have come that you may have life and have it abundantly. I am the good shepherd; the good shepherd gives his life for his sheep".[335]

The more we walk with the Master of the Masters, the more personal experiences we will have with Him and the more our faith will be strengthened. We can expect from God the supply of everything we need, because no hair falls from a Christian's head without God's permission. Nothing is impossible for the believer.[336][337]

On one occasion, I was very troubled and I was hurt by some people, not understanding the reason to encounter certain obstacles in life. Once, when I was waking up from a night's sleep, I distinctly heard in my mind the biblical passage that states that our struggle is not against flesh and blood. Although I knew that biblical passage, I only made the association with my particular situation when I received that divine message, which was true for me at that time, having been instrumental in my Christian walk, because I was able to rework my feelings and channel them correctly.[338]

In the search for divine presence, we can assume two positions that do not find shelter in the Word of God. God is not pleased with settled faith or superficial faith.

Going to meet God does not in any way translate a accommodated faith. Faith is not a philosophical concept to live better, but it is a mental certainty that God will operate personally in the lives of His children, with direct repercussions on the psychological, mental, physical life and attitude and the lives of those around Him.

Science shows that people live longer and better when they believe in the existence of a higher being. However, it is not this faith that people need to have in order to save themselves and have an abundant life. We need to believe in the divine plan of salvation through Jesus Christ. Therefore, saving faith is very specific.

There is no faith in those who simply quickly conform to their adverse situation and everything that goes wrong around them, because they assume that this is in the will of God. It is up to the Christian to make known all his petitions before God and also to do everything in his power to contribute to change. Often the divine response is not instantaneous and it is important that there be prayer from the believer and, if possible, from more believers gathered together. Of course, the Christian must ask for discernment, because the divine answers can be one of the following: "yes", "no", "wait" or "I have something better for you". God's answer is not always affirmative and we have to be prepared to receive it, but Jesus taught us to be the importunate friend and to pray constantly.[339]

What can illustrate the true search of the Christian is the episode of the healing of the paralytic in Capernaum. Jesus had already been to Capernaum, where he had performed many miracles. When four friends of the paralytic learned that Jesus was back in Capernaum, they made a stand to carry their friend to Jesus. They went to the house where He was. As they could not approach the house by the door, because of the crowd, they climbed up and made a hole in the roof of the house through which they lowered the paralytic's bed. [340]

If the four friends had a "accommodating faith", nothing would have happened. But they did everything in their power! It required the agreement of four people, whose attitude reveals that they were true friends of the paralytic. It took four people to transport the patient. Having seen the crowd around the house, they did not give up, decided to raise the stand to the roof, which must have been very painful. Then they had to open the roof and lower the platform to the room where Jesus was.

God wants the participation of Christians in his work and the part of the Christian is to develop a dynamic faith, being sure that God will give the necessary provision to achieve all the objectives that are in accordance with the Word. It is important for every Christian to do what is within his reach.

We realize that what we call "accommodating faith" is nothing more than unbelief. One simply makes the petition to God as if by a conscience disenchantment, but doubt assails his mind.

The superficial faith is not deeply supported in the Holy Scriptures. One believes in some points of the Bible, but does not seek to grow and direct faith from the Word of God. The Bible reports that the Jews of Berea were more noble than those of Thessalonica, for they received the Word earnestly, and every day searched the Scriptures to see if everything was accurate.[341]

Do not accept a speech just because it has been presented by some religious scholar, but always examine what has been said in the light of the Word.

Always turn to the source of God's word, which is the Bible, either to compare what you have heard or read, or to receive God's original guidance.

You may argue that the Bible constitutes a book written by several authors at different and distant times, and that many passages are difficult to understand and accept.

It is critical that you overcome these barriers. Accept the Bible as the true Word of God, written by men inspired by Him and always pray for the Holy Spirit to enlighten your reading.

Never stray from this fundamental step of faith. God will be pleased with this, because he will realize that you consider him powerful enough to convey to humanity exactly the message that He wanted to leave on record for people.

Faith should not be molded to reality; is the reality that must be shaped by faith.

Many people adopt a language of unbelief. The Christian should not follow the majority, even because the path of salvation is narrow and few pass through it. [342]

The Scriptures must be examined with the certainty that they contain the truth clearly and directly, without hidden meanings. Seek to read the Word as a child seeking the teachings of the Heavenly Father. Try telling the Biblical story of David and Goliath to a small child and see how simple the child will accept that truth. An adult, devoid of faith, may question the historicity and validity of the report.

Anchor your faith exclusively in the Word of God, which is the Bible, for any other form of belief will only draw you away from God's presence.

It is never enough to repeat that Jesus is the only way to vivify the soul.

Another important point is that God fulfills all His promises without exception. All that is prophesied and promised in the Holy Bible will be fulfilled, because the Almighty has extreme zeal for his Name and for his Word.

If you can have this basic and simple faith and seek the Kingdom of God above all things, you will begin to see things happen in your life.

The Bible is the general manual of God's will. There are contained ordinances and general promises. The moment I accept God's sonship and hear the preaching, God will communicate to your child his specific will. For example, opening the Red Sea was a specific will for Moses, but most likely it will not be for you today. Jesus determined that the disciples should go into the whole world (Mark 16:15); It was also a specific will for those disciples and a general will for other readers, but it may not be a specific will for you today. Maybe God wants you to evangelize your community, starting with your neighbors.

If you know God's specific will and it has been communicated to you, the first requirement for God's supernatural action to take place is met. The second requirement is faith: God has already approved your provision, it is enough that you take it by faith.

That is a biblical truth and not an invention. The Lord Jesus said that it is enough faith the size of a mustard seed - the smallest existing grain - for a mountain to throw itself into the sea.

Is it that simple? Affirmative.

Many people despise Jesus not only for their unbelief, but also because of the peaceful nature of His teachings and the form of death He suffered.

He who does not identify in the life and offering of Jesus Christ the values inherent in the character of God, and holds them in the highest regard, will never be able to understand the reasons why he was sent and why he spontaneously gave himself up to be crucified.

God seeks true worshipers, that is, worshipers who are faithful to Him. And Jesus came to fulfill the mission of salvation and demonstrated fidelity to the last moment. Jesus zealously ensured that all the prophecies were fulfilled and so loved the world that he gave his life for many.

It is a misconception of the language of unbelief to think that Christians find themselves unprotected and that it is only up to them to accept suffering and aggression without reacting.

It was not so that the apostle Paul who, on more than one occasion, invoked his Roman citizenship to rid himself of adversity. [343]

In the spiritual world, things happen to the extent of our faith. God has already given us His Word and the righteous live simply by faith. The Christian is by no means powerless in this world; On the contrary, their faith can unleash the supernatural action of God.

Suffering must be seen as something positive, because through it we develop our faith, and certainly no harm will come to us without God's permission and never above our own strength.

We will be protected from the attacks of the Enemy, when our faith is grounded in God.

In the foreground, the Holy Spirit strengthens our defenses against sin and we can freely choose to follow God's ways.

As for the most ostentatious attacks of the Devil, which provoke infirmities, oppressions and possessions in people, so God does not leave us orphans.

I have learned from various experiences that evil oppressions also affect (and mainly) believers, but fervent prayer - for which liberation is called by invoking the name of Jesus - is fully effective!

Oppression afflicted me constantly and, not infrequently, I felt successive attacks, which required several firm prayers. We can ask that God rebuke Satan or the spirit that is afflicting us and that we be delivered from oppression in the name of Jesus, because God is all-powerful and there is no magic or satanic power that can overcome Him. The Beloved Apostle exults: "He who is with us is greater than he who is in the world!" Even successive attacks of oppression can be repulsed with specific prayers, or with rebukes proper to the spirits of darkness, including casting them into the abyss.[34][35][36]

Jesus' promise is clear: "Whatever you ask for with faith in prayer, you will receive it". Thus, he who does not doubt in his heart, can ask anything of God, provided, of course, the request is in accordance with God's will (in the above case, it will always be). [347]

It is common for Christians themselves to brush certain Biblical passages and form a "personal Bible", since it is much more convenient to ignore the "difficult part" of the Bible, which affects us directly and personally.

Christ has bequeathed to us his words, which are truth and life for today and ever, as timely for our day as they were 2,000 years ago. To believe in Jesus is to accept his revolutionary gospel and be willing to follow it in all circumstances.

I remember now the question that someone close to me asked me: "Why have Jesus?" "To have peace", I answered. And he wrote "but I already have peace".

I could have concluded that I did not refer to the peace that earthly life can bring, such as the lack of conflict with other people, or the tranquility that we can have when everything goes well with us from a material and physical point of view (finance and health, e.g. in the words of Jesus, his peace exceeds all understanding. Consequently, no one can adequately express this state of grace in words.

I will try, however, within my experience, to relate what the peace of Christ has brought me:

- conviction of the forgiveness of sins;

- certainty of having been accepted by God and belonging to Him;

- conviction of being on the right track;

- conviction to be saved;

- knowledge of the goodness and love of God;

- understanding that earthly life is only the anteroom of what is to come;

- finally, conviction of the truth.

One may also object that the Christian life is very difficult, as it requires many renunciations and dedication. In fact, the Christian life is the narrow way that leads to salvation, but on this journey we are not alone or abandoned to our own fate, because Christ goes with us, in front of us, to assure us victory whatever the kind of mishap and under all circumstances. [348]

Finally, the peace of Christ raises us to a level where the setbacks and disappointments of earthly life fail to reach us as before and we no longer have the same concern for life. All these old occupations and worries move into a secondary position in our thoughts and in our life.

Peace, which exceeds all understanding, is only one aspect of life with Christ. The Christian experiences an extreme transformation in his life, becoming what the Bible calls a "new creature".

6.4 Sanctifying

Simply believing in the Bible as God's inspired work is not enough for us to be considered righteous before God, because demons believe and tremble before God Almighty.[349]

Do we, then, need to possess something more than simple faith? The answer is surely affirmative in the light of the authority of the Bible.

We have already dealt with, in the chapters "

The commandments of God The commandments in the teaching of Jesus

The situation contrary to life in sin is sanctified life.

Strictly speaking, only the Most High is Holy completely; If there is a degree of holiness, we can say that the only God is so in his most absolute, exalted and full expression. The Word of God tells us:

"No one is holy like the Lord,

There is none beside thee." (BTE, 1. Samuel 2:2)

"For thus speaketh the high and high,

who inhabits eternity and whose name is holy." (BTE, Isaiah 57:15).

The Most High expects us also to seek sanctification:

"For I am the LORD your God: ye shall therefore sacrifice yourselves to be holy, for I am holy: I have not made you yourselves unclean with all these beasts that swarm and swarm upon the earth. For I am the LORD that brought you up out of the land of Egypt, that I may be God unto you: ye must therefore be holy; for I am holy." (Bte, Leviticus 11:44-45)

"The LORD spake unto Moses, saying, Speak unto all the congregation of the children of

Israel, and thou shalt say unto them, Be holy; for I am holy, I the LORD your God." (Leviticus 19:1-2, BTE)

One of the most exciting themes for Christendom and the core of our faith concerns Christian freedom in the face of the need for sanctification.

When it comes to this subject, one has to resort to Paul's epistles which most profoundly talked about him.

Rather, however, it should be borne in mind that the Pauline epistles do not innovate, nor do they conflict with the teachings of Jesus, although the Apostle Paul has coined meanings specific to some words always ingeniously, to the point of attributing to the apostle Paul the doctrinal formatting of Christianity.

The Church of Christ was and always will be the same; it moves in function of the person of Jesus, and not of another apostle however important it might have been.

Indubitably, the Apostle Paul contributed, as few and in a remarkable way, to the propagation of the Gospel and to the understanding of the teaching of Jesus, creating specific terminologies for existing realities and explaining, in a peculiar way, the truths that Jesus bequeathed to us.

Therefore, there is no "doctrine" as a different creation from the truth of Christ. The apostle Paul in no way produced any change in the "set of principles that govern... the dogmas of a religion." What distinguishes the Apostle Paul is his own method of explaining a truth already known and previously revealed by Jesus.[350]

This point is fundamental to any Bible study, remembering that the teaching of Jesus corresponds to the authentic interpretation of that Word, that is, interpretation in which the applicator is confused with the author of the Word (=law).

For the apostle Paul, sanctification translates into resistance to sin. It is Paul who, supporting Jesus, teaches that the practice of sin leads to spiritual death.

What sin, however, is Paul referring to? Can your concept be subjectivated, according to each one's consciousness?

The Pauline epistles can be understood perfectly when their **purely theoretical** basis *is subordinated* to Paul's practical understanding of sin and sanctification.

Paul never indulged in the practice of sin, having severely attacked idolatry, theft, adultery, covetousness, theft, murder, dishonor of father and mother, perjury, and all other sins.[351][352][353][354][355][356][357][358][359]

Note that Paul goes beyond the Decalogue to condemn sins foreseen in other passages of the Pentateuch, such as: magic, homosexuality and lesbianism, rebelliousness against parents, marital relations between the stepmother and stepson and prostitution.[360][361][362][363][364][365]

Paul also catalogues as sins: debauchery contrary to the purity of the body, debauchery and orgies, lies, hatred, jealousy, discord, anger, rivalries, dissensions and factions, greed for profit or greed, greed, wickedness, wickedness and envy.[366][367][368][369][370][371][372][373][374][375][376][377][378]

He also reproached the effeminate and the pederasts, the thieves, the greedy and drunkards, the slanderers and revilers, the rapacious and the slave traders.[379][380][381][382]

Paul placed special emphasis on purification, recommending to believers chastity and to turn away: from fornicators, greedy, idolaters, rapaciouss, slanderers, drunkards, thieves, or those who had a disorderly life or contrary to tradition. He also condemned the impurity of the body caused by the lust of hearts.[383][384][385][386]

From this practical thought of Paul we can appreciate the theoretical basis of his epistles.

Paul, therefore, showed himself to be an extremely zealous man in observing the divine commandments, coming from the Decalogue and the Pentateuch, with the temperaments and aggravating brought by Jesus, of which we have already occupied ourselves in the chapter "The commandments in the teaching of Jesus". The commandments in the teaching of Jesus

After all Paul brought his Pharisaic baggage from the tribe of Benjamin, having been instructed at the feet of Gamaliel, who was a doctor of the law, according to his exactness.[387][388][389][390]

Paul was an extremely energetic and idealistic man. Before his conversion, he persecuted believers relentlessly as an inquisitor, even torturing them so that they could blaspheme and be stoned to death, or even issued suffrage to provoke the death of Christians.[391]

Paul's practical position, as a staunch follower of the divine commandments, seems to oppose the doctrine of justification by grace.

This subject involves much controversy among the various Christian denominations, while some emphasize that the believer is justified by faith, others highlight the need for the practice of works and the third understand justification is by combining faith and works.

It was Paul who most developed the doctrine of grace, and the following verse is well known:

> "For you are saved by grace through faith, and that not of yourselves; it is the gift of God; Not of works, lest any man should boast." (Ephesians 2:8-9, BTE)

The doctrine of grace has been misinterpreted by many to the extent that they held that the law had lapsed and that the believer was exempt from keeping the commandments. Hence it is said that Paul would not be "legalistic".

I recently watched a television programme in which a religious leader of a denomination who considers himself Christian participated. He claimed that Jesus attracted all people's past and future sins, and now they were free to do whatever they wanted.

The Bible, however, nowhere does it support such a conclusion. What was unclean and abominable to God in the time of Moses remains in the times of today.

See that the Master Jesus, being Son Sent with all authority received from the Father, granted us one . Authentic interpretation of God's will It is authentic because the interpretation is made by the Divine Entity itself (Heavenly Council) from which the divine Word originated. When a judge applies the law, he makes an interpretation of the precept edited by other people (legislators). Therefore, if hypothetically there was a contradiction between the gospels and another writing, the eventual divergence should always be interpreted in favor of the former. [392]

The doctrinal unity of the New Testament is, like the Pauline epistles, based on the teachings of Jesus.

Someone has already said that the discussion ends when we define the concepts. So it is with the terminology Paulina. Understanding the meaning of the terms with which the Apostle Paul so well expresses himself, such as fruits, works, righteousness, grace, and law, are fundamental to understanding the rich ministry of St. Paul.

Let us first take grace in its traditional meaning, as synonymous with the free gift of God for the pious (mercy).

Notice that the expression mercy involves the action of two people: God, who makes his appreciation and can pity, and the suffering person who repents of his sinful life (faith plus repentance).[393]

Grace, in the sense of divine mercy, has always been an element of justification, even in the times of the first covenant, not having been introduced as novelty by Jesus (in his earthly existence).

Indeed, Jesus condemned the essence of the law to three aspects: mercy (love), justice and faithfulness.[394]

Thus, we can see in the Bible that Noah was a man who found grace before God, just as Moses also achieved it.[395][396]

It is easy to understand justification by grace, by faith in Jesus, in the case of the newly converted. However, difficulties begin to arise when one takes into account that, normally, this convert will have a whole life ahead of him and the question arises: does he not need to have works? Or can he remain in his condition as a sinner-sufferer within an eternal circle of repentance-forgiveness? [397]

Paul considering this situation, was led to exclaim, "Unhappy with me! Who will release me from this body of death?" Then having the glimpse of the solution: "Grace be given to God through Jesus Christ our Lord" (Romans 8:24, Jerusalem Bible).

In this final part of the verse, Paul released a clarification regarding his concept of grace, which is not that taken from the Old Testament (= mercy, only).

Paul adds one more component to the grace that can be called the free gift of Christ's life in us. Thus, Paul raises supplication to God:

"that with his glorious riches he may strengthen you in the depths of your being with power through the Spirit, that Christ may dwell in your hearts through faith; and I pray that, being rooted and grounded in love, you may, together with all the saints, comprehend the breadth, length, height, and depth, and know the love of Christ which surpasses all knowledge, that you may be filled with all the fullness of God." (Ephesians 3:16 to 19 in the Bible)

Paul considered grace sufficient for justification, by the fact that his concept of grace also embraced the new birth by the Divine Spirit and not only mercy, as can be drawn from the following passages:

"Now therefore there is no more condemnation to them which are of the law of the Spirit which giveth life, he hath delivered me from the law and from sin." (Romans 8:1-2) em Jesus Cristo. Poisem Jesus Cristo

"But if we are dead with Christ, we believe that we shall also live with him." (Romans 6:8, BTE)

Notice that there is no newness in this, for the Saviour teaches that only he who is born from on high and those who remain in him will attain salvation, associating the Vine with him and the branches with believers. [398]

Returning to the subject of freedom, it was Paul who developed it the most, but no one has explained freedom as concisely and magnificently as the Deliverer himself, who is Jesus:

> "Jesus said therefore to the Jews who had believed on him, 'If you remain in my word', you are truly my disciples, you will know the truth and the truth will make you free men." They answered him, "We are Abraham's seed, and no man reduced us to bondage; How can you expect us to become free men?" Jesus answered them, "Verily, verily, I say unto you, He that committeth sin is the servant of sin. The slave does not always remain in the house; But the son abideth in him for ever. If therefore the Son sets you free, you are truly free men" (John 8:31 to 36, BTE)[399]

The relationship between the new birth and sanctification is direct, as Paul teaches:

> "When you were slaves to sin, you were free in relation to righteousness. What fruits did you produce then? Being ashamed of them today, for their end is death. But now, freed from sin and made slaves of Christ, produce the fruits that lead to sanctification and whose end is eternal life."

The Christian is delivered from the inclination to sin by being born of the Spirit, according to the account contained in the book of John:

> "Now there was among the Pharisees a man named Nicodemus, one of the notable Jews. He came to Jesus by night and said to him: «Rabbi, we know that you are a teacher who comes from God, for no one can work the signs that you do unless God is with him. 'Jesus answered him, "Verily, verily, I say unto thee, Unless he be born again, no man can see the kingdom of God." Nicodemus said to him: How could a man be born when he was old? Could he enter a second time into his mother's bosom and be born?" Jesus answered him, Verily, verily, I say unto thee, Except a man be born of water and of the Spirit, he cannot enter into the kingdom of God. That which is born of the flesh is flesh, and that which is born of the Spirit is spirit. Do not be surprised because I said: You must be born from above. The wind blows where it wants, and you hear its voice, but you don't know where it comes from or where it goes. So it is with everyone who is born of the Spirit. '" (BTE, John 3:1-8) [400]

> For Paul, who was born again through Christ is a new creature **and is symbolically** dead to sins **as** if the old man had been crucified with Jesus:

"Therefore, if anyone is in Christ, he is a new creature. The old world is gone, behold, there is a new reality." (BTE, 2nd Corinthians 5:17)

"Let us understand this well: our old man was crucified with him, that this body of sin may be destroyed, and that we may no longer be slaves to sin. For he that is dead is delivered from sin. But if we are dead with Christ, we believe that we shall also live with him... Likewise you also consider that you are dead to sin and alive to God in Christ Jesus. " (BTE, Romans 6:6-11)

The new birth of the Spirit is the most important milestone of Christian life and consists of supernatural experience with God.

The light and love of God reach us so intensely in the new birth that we replace our old thoughts and bad habits with the noble and positive feelings that the Most High pours on those who are his and who seek him sincerely, such as love, compassion, Benevolence, humility, sweetness, patience, according to Colossians 3:12 and 14.

We are born again to walk in newness **of life. In the happy**[401] expression of the apostle Paul: "those who belong to Christ crucified the flesh with their passions and desires. If we live by the Spirit, let us also walk under the impulse of the Spirit."

As the Apostle Paul writes:

> "The works of the flesh are well known: debauchery, uncleanness, debauchery, idolatry, magic, hatred, discord, jealousy, anger, rivalries, dissensions, factions, envy, drunkenness, orgies, and the like; The authors of these things, I warn you, as I have said, shall not inherit the kingdom of God." (BTE, Galatians 5:19-21)

The apostle Paul opposes the inclination of the flesh to life in the Spirit and does so by supporting Jesus. It seems to us that the passage conveys that, without being born again in Christ, we cannot abandon sin forever. The flesh may not be naturally sinful, but human selfishness and lust cause it to sin. It is opportune to remember that the folly of man associated with his intellectual autonomy also helps to explain the choices that man makes to turn away from God, as we treat in chapter of this work. [402]

I may want to be nice, good, kind, quiet, for example, but, at my core, I don't feel all this well-being and circumstances can make me try to force a behavior that is not characteristic to me. Thus, I pass only one appearance of what I am, and not my essence. Of course it is very easy to be good and kind to those who give us reciprocity.

The new life which the Divine Spirit gives to believers consists in the spontaneous **observance of the divine commandments and the freedom** of the believer becomes the coincidence between **the will of God and that of God.**

Thus the Christian finds deliverance from the principle that leads him to sin, breaking the circle - once endless - of sin-repentance-sin. Sin, for the Christian, becomes an accident of course: he no longer lives as a slave to sin.

We fulfill the commandments not because it is an obligation imposed, but because we receive the mind of Christ by the new birth and have joy and pleasure in observing the divine ordinances, which are the reason for the upliftment of our soul.

We stopped being servants to be adopted Sons of the Most High. Jesus is the Bread and Water of Life, which strengthens us daily and will remain with us until the end of the age. Jesus is always with us spiritually, He being the head of His invisible Church, while the faithful are the members of the body. Or: Jesus is the Vine and the branches are those that remain with Him. [403] [404] [405] [406] [407]

It is the Heavenly Council, therefore, that sanctifies us with its presence in our lives, so that we come to reflect the holy character of God.

Paul refuses to see, in this process of sanctification, the participation of the believer: the fruits come as a consequence of the connection to Christ; the believer cannot glory in himself or claim to be justified by his own efforts (works). God pleases us both with willing and effectual. [408] [409]

This recurrent point of Paul throughout his work - inspired by the Most High -, seems to be explained by the extraordinary and profound conversion of Paul and his intimate communion with Jesus. However, it seems that the Apostle Paul cannot completely and logically close his reasoning.

Note that the connection with Christ, which is the concept of grace for Paul, depends on a reciprocity of the believer. He must *abide* in Christ.

As discussed in the second chapter, the Most High endowed the human being with intellectual autonomy, by reason of which he assumes direct responsibility for his obedience or disobedience, which consists in remaining under the lordship of Christ or rejecting him.

Communion with Jesus, which is a two-way street, is established and perpetuated as long as the Master's words and love remain with us:

> "I am the true vine, and my Father is the vineyard. Every man that bringeth forth fruit in me, he bringeth it forth, and every man that bringeth forth fruit, he pruneth it, purifieth it, that it may bring forth more. You are already purified by the word I have told you. Remain in me as I remain in you! Even as Armento cannot bear fruit of himself, except he abide in the vine, so also ye, except ye abide in the vineyard, are the branches: he that abideth in me, and in him in whom I abide, he shall bring forth fruit in abundance: for being cut off from me: nothing you can do. If anyone does not abide in me, he is thrown away, like Armento, and dries up; And they are gathered together, and are cast into the fire, and burn. If ye abide in me, and my words abide in you, ye shall ask what ye will, and it shall be granted you. What glorifies my Father is that you bring forth fruit in abundance and become my disciples. As the Father has loved me, so have I loved you: remain in my love. If ye

keep my commandments, ye shall abide in my love, as I abide in my love by the commandments of my Father" (John 15:1-10, BTE).

Jesus taught that whoever is in Him produces much fruit and continues to produce much fruit whoever remains in Him. What is this fruit but the fruit of the Holy Spirit?

The fruit is very different from works. While the fruit is spontaneously generated by the vine, the works are the efforts of each one, carried out even against his own nature. Therefore to abide in Christ means to abide with the mind of Christ; means to remain under the lordship of Jesus. This implies sanctification.

Those who read the Pauline epistles attentively will see that Paul, far from preaching the freedom to sin, urges readers to sanctify themselves, to practice righteousness, and to produce much fruit:

"And then what? Are we to sin because we are no longer under the law, but under grace? No, of course not! Know ye not, that, putting yourselves in the service of a man as a slave to obey him, ye are slaves to him whom ye obey, whether of sin, which leads to death, or of obedience, which leads to righteousness? Let us give thanks to God: you were slaves to sin, but you obeyed with all your heart the common teaching to which you were entrusted; Freed from sin, you have become slaves to righteousness. I use words totally human, adapted to your weaknesses. In the same way that you have made your members slaves in the service of uncleanness and disorder, which lead to revolt against God, now making them slaves to the service of righteousness, which leads to sanctification. When you were slaves to sin, you were free in relation to righteousness. What fruits did you produce then? Today you are ashamed of them, for their end is death. But now freed from sin and made slaves of God, produce the fruits that lead to sanctification and whose end is eternal life. For the wages of sin is death; But the gift of God is eternal life, our Lord." (Romans 6:15-23, BTE)

One of the most beautiful words of Jesus is found in John 8:31-36:

"Then said Jesus unto the Jews which believed on him, If ye continue in my word, ye shall be my disciples indeed, and know the truth, and the truth shall make you free. 'They answered, 'We are the seed of Abraham and we are no one's slaves. How can you say, 'Ye shall be free'? Jesus answered them, Verily, verily, I say unto you, He that committeth sin is a bondservant. Now the slave does not always remain in the house, but the son remains there forever. If

The freedom that Christ offers us, by grace, is that our will and our accomplishment, by grace and divine provision, come to coincide with the will of God. We receive the mind of Christ. Thus, we are free when we commit ourselves to keep God's commandments, because what we desire and what we do is just what God wants us to do! We are not seeking to keep the commandments because we simply fear the sanction of the law, but mainly because God has transformed our lives and our hearts and impressed upon them His ordinances. The Christian is pleased to keep the commandments, for this is also the desire of his heart, and therein lies his freedom; he will never do anything at the service of the passions of the flesh.

If it is true that God gives us both will and effect, there is always in the Christian attitude and practice a letting oneself be led by [410]*Christ in the use of* the intellectual autonomy of the believer, which is revealed in various ways: public affirmation of Jesus and his lordship; sharing Christ with others; prayer; reading the Word of God; philanthropy; application in the fulfillment of the divine commandments.

The apostle Paul introduces a new view of the law, arguing that although holy, the knowledge of it would give occasion to all kinds of lusts and sin would take life. But if God had not given us the commandments, how would we know how to please and worship him? Pagan peoples, even without the law, have not ceased to sin, finding themselves totally separated from the one God, beginning with the practice of idolatry. The Hebrews themselves, from Abraham to the Exodus, had not received the legal detailing that began with Moses, nor were they holier than the Jews who were under the Mosaic Law. [411]

Paul's statement has to do with the fallen nature of man, who is rebellious against the will of God, although this is good, holy, and just. That is, the law produces in the Carnal Man the desire to break it. [412]

So much so that the apostle Paul writes that sin is in its members and dwells within, in explaining that its members (the flesh) would be in conflict with its spirit and with the law. [413]

No doubt Paul transmitted that Christians cannot be justified before God by virtue of their own merits (works), since no Man has attained perfection, and they will only be justified if and as long as they remain in Christ, which accredits them to produce the fruits of righteousness. [414]

It is interesting that Paul uses the word "fruit" well, *as* did the Master Jesus Christ, differentiating them from "works". While the works result from the will and exclusive commitment of the human being; the fruit is born naturally of the new character of the people who are in Christ, so that believers produce fruit and are associated with the branches that are united to the Vine, which is Christ. The fruits are produced with the help of Jesus. Therefore, the interpretation of the passage Paulina on justification by grace and not by works, must be understood in light of the meaning of these expressions for Paul.

James, oblivious to Paul's conceptual subtleties in distinguishing between works of fruit, writes about the works that must accompany every believer:

> "My brothers, what good is it to say that you have faith if you have no works? Can faith save

in this case? If a brother or sister has nothing to wear and what to eat every day, and one of you says to them: Go in peace, be warm, have a good appetite! Without, however, giving them the necessary to survive, what would be the point? Likewise, faith that had no works would be dead in its isolation. But a man shall say, Ye have faith; I also have works. Prove unto me thy faith without works, that I will take away my faith out of my works. Believest thou that God is one? Thou doest well. Devils also believe, and tremble. '" (James 2:14-20, BTE)

Paul always emphasizes that we have been reached by grace and our Christian walk is the result of the fruit resulting from the new nature in Christ. Finally, everything is a consequence of the grace of God, including our faith, which comes by hearing the Word and is a gift of God.

Sanctification involves primarily divine help, but it does not dispense with the will and posture of the believer.

While God produces sanctification in the believer, it is up to him to preserve and confirm, at every moment, this divine gift by making use of his intellectual autonomy.

The Lord God did not program people to act like robots, who render blind obedience to pre-established commands. He did so to prove the faithfulness of each one, since He seeks people who worship Him in spirit and in truth.

The Lord God, through Christ, communicates to us his Holiness through the fruit of the Holy Spirit: love, joy, peace, patience, goodness, benevolence, faith, sweetness and self-control.[415]

Holiness, therefore, can be understood as the process during which Christ purifies us and enables us to obey the will of God. But in order for Christ to remain in us we must have recorded His words in our minds and in our hearts, and the words of Christ are prompted that we should apply ourselves to the fulfillment **of the commandments** and that His coming did not matter in repeal of the law and the prophets.

Perhaps one of the happiest and most faithful translations of the Bible is found in the Ecumenical Bible Translation, which reads:

> "If ye love me, ye shall do my commandments." (John 14:15)

> "He that holdeth fast to my commandments, and keepeth them, he loveth me: and he that loveth me shall be loved of my Father, and I will

in turn love him, and will shew myself unto him." (John 14:21)

The true worship and faithfulness of those who seek God is translated into spontaneous attachment to the commandments of Christ.

Note that even the good use of the word "fruits of justice" by Paul does not exclude autonomy . Christian's intellectual, at every moment, decide in accordance with the teachings of Jesus, at the risk of the branch being cut off and thrown into the fire[416]

Sanctification involves primarily divine help, but it does not dispense with the will and posture of the believer.

Notice the reader that the Paulin expression that the believer is "dead to sin" is equivalent to the spontaneous fulfillment of God's commandments. It doesn't matter that I use the form of a commission (to practice justice) or the omissive form (not to sin). Likewise, there is no difference in calling the commandments "laws and prophets", or calling them "righteousness", since the expressions are equivalent to opposing "sins", so much so that the Lord Jesus employed both words.

Paul preferred to use the word "righteousness" rather than "law" and had his reasons.

For Paul, the practice of "righteousness" was the common denominator between Jews and Gentiles, since the latter were not legally subject to the rule of Jewish law; after all, the latter were not Jews. Since the criterion of justification is the same for Gentiles and Jews and the law only required them, it defends the practice of righteousness, but as the new character from which it received grace, not considering it as the cause of justification.

Justice must accompany every Christian, seeming that the discussion of whether it is cause or effect is only a doctrinal subtlety.

Paul also invoked the fact that the strict application of the justice derived from the Mosaic law would lead everyone to eternal damnation.[417]

Another reason that made Paul prefer the expression "righteousness" rather than "law" is that Christians will not be subjected to the final judgment, since they will pass from death to life. This fact - revealed by Jesus - is used by Paul to maintain that justification has no cause in the law. This is in accordance with the teachings of Jesus as to the believer's non-subjection to the final judgment. As for the judgment of the pagans, Paul, praising the revelation of Jesus and the passage inserted in Psalm 62:13, states that God "will render to every man according to his works" what He confers with the teaching of Jesus.[418] [419] [420] [421] [422]

Paul glimpsed that Jesus had withdrawn the authority of men, before bestowed by the Mosaic law, to denounce, judge, condemn their fellow men, and apply the sanctions provided by the law in the name of God.

This can be clearly extracted from the episode of the adulterous woman:

> "They went every man to his house, and Jesus went into the mount of Olives. And when it was day, he returned into the temple: and all the people came unto him, and sat down, and taught. The scribes and the Pharisees then brought a woman who had been surprised in adultery and posted her in the midst of the group. Master, they told them, this woman was caught in the act of adultery. In the law, Moses commanded us to stone such women. What do you say about that? They talked like that with the intention of setting him up, so I had to

accuse him. But Jesus, stooping down, began to write with his finger traces on the ground. As they continued to ask him questions, Jesus stood up and said to them, Whosoever of you never sinned, cast the first stone at him. And, leaning, he began again to write traces on the ground. After they had heard these words, they withdrew one after another, starting with their elders, and Jesus was left alone. As the woman stood there in the middle of the circle, Jesus stood up and said to her: Woman, where are they? ' Has no one condemned you? 'She answered, Nobody, Lord. 'And Jesus said to her, 'Neither do I condemn you: go, and sin no more. '" (John 8:1-11)

The Jews received the ordinances directly from God, who were endowed with sanction against noncompliance with the precepts; therefore, it is certain that they had the force of a perfect law (standard + sanction).

These divine commandments received the legal garb of law.

No human society can be considered civilized if relations between its members and from them to the government are not at all established in such a way as to guarantee a good coexistence and a just solution of the conflicts of interest that will naturally arise.

Well, the act that regulates these relations is called, in law, legal norm and the garment that this legal norm receives is called law.

Santiago Dantas already said that the perfect legal norm is only one endowed with sanction. People are obliged to conform their conduct to the terms of the law, under penalty of suffering the outbreak of consequences and punishments that radiate from it. [423]

The sanction acts in two ways: preventive and concrete. At first, the advertising of the norm acts in the psychic sphere of people and aims to warn them about the consequences (sanction) caused by the breach of the precept. This usually produces the will and interest to shape their behavior to the precepts of the law. Hence why the beginning of the existence of the law coincides with its publication, so that no one can excuse himself from its fulfillment by alleging ignorance. In a second moment, when an act contrary to the norm has been practised, the penalty is applied to a specific case.

From Christ, the Lord God came to inhabit the body of the faithful according to 1 Corinthians 6:15 and 19 which form the Church of Christ. The tabernacle became the body of the faithful and God dwells in the people. God is personal. [424][425]

Now, the followers of Christ no longer submitted to the rule of law, understood from the juridical point of view, as the regulator of social life, because the Son of God removed an element implicit in the concept of law: sanction. He did this when he removed the authority of men to judge and condemn his fellows in the name of God. Jesus also taught that we will be judged with the same severity with which we judge others.

What is justice for Saint Paul? It consists of the precepts contained in the Jewish law, unveiled, however, of its legal garb (= prohibitions). The law loses its coercive and retributive nature (sanction) and becomes precepts of justice, observed spontaneously by Christians.

Nor could it be different, because God's commandments are rules of happiness for the human spirit.

The Psalmist exclaims "Lord, show me the way of your decrees, and my reward will be to observe them. Give me understanding, and I will keep your law, and will keep it with all my heart. Lead me in the way of your commandments, for in this I find pleasure... yes, I love your precepts; for your justice, make me live again". (Psalm 119:33-40)

It is God himself who associates holiness with the observance of his precepts:

> "The LORD your God commands you today to follow these decrees and ordinances; obey them attentively, with all their heart and with all their soul. Today you have declared that the LORD is your God and that you will walk in his ways, that you will keep his decrees, his commandments, and his ordinances, and that you will obey him. And today the LORD has declared that you are his people, his special treasure, as he promised, and that you will have to obey all the commandments. He has declared that he will give you a position of glory, fame, and honor far above all the nations he has made, and that you will be a holy people to the LORD your GOD, as he promised."

Holiness involves a continuous affirmation of our intellectual autonomy in favor of Christ and the will of God. The Lord God does not compel us to seek righteousness; He provides us with enough weapons to achieve it in our daily lives, and it is up to us to decide whether or not to remain in it.

If you accept Christ in our lives, you certainly have a wonderful experience with God. From this, the Christian must persevere in the faith and remain with Christ and in his Light.

If we call ourselves Christians, but despise our parents and our neighbor, what is the confrontation we are making between Christianity and our conduct?

The Disciple of love warns us to say that we pass as liars when we despise our neighbor, who is under our sight, and we think we love God, whom we do not see (1 John 4:20).

Jesus teaches us that sin is darkness and everyone who loves God sincerely seeks to live in the Light. God is Light, love, righteousness, and all those who love the Light spontaneously abandon the darkness of sin.

> "There is no eternal condemnation reserved for those who trust in Him as Savior. But those who do not trust Him have already been judged and condemned for not believing in God's only Son. Their sentence is based on this fact: the Light from heaven came into the world, but they loved darkness more than Light, because their works were evil. They hated the heavenly Light because they wanted to sin in the darkness. They stayed away from that Light, afraid that their sins would be revealed and they would be punished. But those who behave well, take

To live pleasantly in the Light is to have a sincere desire to serve God righteously, forsaking sin, and this implies observing the divine precepts, because it is they who enlighten us about sin and about life in fellowship with God.

The fulfillment of the divine law ceases to be a painful and imposed task for those who seek to live in the light of Jesus and are aware that the law of God is good and beautiful and aims to bring happiness to man. Whoever lives in the Light does not need to strive to produce fruit. They arise spontaneously, which distinguishes them from the works, which are the product of human effort and intelligence.

6.5 *Renewing the mind and heart*

We are what we think. Ralph Waldo Emerson used to say that "man is what he thinks all the time".[426]

It is the quality of our thinking that determines our spontaneous outward manifestations, that is, those that come from our heart, not concealed. Jesus teaches that man speaks spontaneously of things the heart is full of according to Matthew 12:34-35.[427]

When one cherishes useless and unpleasant thoughts within, it is natural that this mental habit will reverberate in the mind and, consequently, in the conduct and in the mood.

Remember that everything begins in the mind, including sin. It is our mind that coordinates all our thoughts. If we cannot control our mind, we cannot restrain our tongue.[428]

We are in sin when we do not devote our worship and praise to the One God. The first great commandment in Jesus' teaching is, "Love the Lord your God with all your heart, and with all your soul, and with all your mind." (BNVI, Matthew 22:37)

Loving wholeheartedly involves a sincere desire for communion and closeness to God. When our heart is devoted to God, whenever we raise our thoughts to him, we have all sorts of noble feelings.

Loving God of all understanding also says with the acceptance of divine sovereignty and its purposes and purposes.

Loving God with the whole soul presupposes the cultivation of biblical truths in the mind and the desire to be permanently conformed to them.

How much of the Bible do we know, and what portion of the Bible do we believe in? We should read the Bible by pointing out the passages we consider most important.

The Scriptures teach us how we are to worship God, and this matter was detailed in Chapter 3 of this work ("The Commandments of God"), to which we refer. Basically, the Lord God commands us to worship only the Living God; prohibits us from making images; prohibits the attitude of worship of other gods; prohibits the pronouncement of God's name in vain.

God's designs are superior to the purposes of men. We are truly worshipping God, when his achievements and designs do not bring us strangeness or perplexity.

To love God, first of all, is to love Jesus, because Jesus came to announce the message of God and to fulfill the prophecies concerning the Messiah.

Whoever does not love Jesus Christ cannot love God the Father, because Christ has revealed to us the will and character of God the Father, as well as the plan of salvation conceived from the creation of the world. [429]

One cannot please God without the awareness of his greatness, of his superiority and of his sovereignty and, on the other hand, of our smallness and transience.

Who are we to question God's will? Some of the Jewish people had the unfortunate habit of complaining against God during the crossing of the desert to Canaan, although God Himself was feeding them with manna for 40 years and directing the People through a pillar of fire. Several were the wonders and miracles which God worked when the Jews were under the leadership of Moses. [430]

The attitude of the Jewish people caused a great delay in arriving in the Promised Land and prevented the Jews of that generation from stepping into Canaan.

We must consider whether we are not also in the habit of attributing the difficulties of life to God. It is common for people themselves to contribute to the emergence of difficulties. It is true that life is not easy for anyone, as it was not for the Jews who had to walk in the desert for 40 years.

The Word of God contains messages of optimism, love, faith, hope and solidarity.

The message that the world divulges is that of the language of hopelessness, centered on the immediate vision of earthly life. For her, the maximum value lies in the safety and comfort that life can provide to some privileged. We must repay love to those who love us well, but impose the respect of the adversaries, following, when possible, the maxim: "hit, took". The language of the world is selfish and self-sufficient. It is centered on man and his institutions.

Christ taught us that we will receive the gifts and blessings in the measure of our faith.

Accepting Jesus means that we are ready to trust the words he has bequeathed to us.

An interesting technique to combat negative thoughts is to continually empty the spirit. Our spirit can be emptied of our fears, of our pessimism, of everything that worries us for a few minutes and then be filled with noble thoughts, good and positive, of self-confidence and self-esteem, rejecting all kinds of negative thinking, unclean and of evil design.

This technique is explained by Norman Vincent Peale:[431]

> "A simple method for acquiring this peace is to practice the spiritual emptying. I will talk about this in another chapter. I mention it here, just to emphasize the importance of a frequent mental catharsis. I recommend that you do the 'soul-emptying' at least twice a day or more if necessary. Seek to purge from it the fear, the hatred, the feeling of insecurity and guilt and the sorrows. The simple fact that you consciously make this effort to empty the spirit tends to provide great relief. Did you ever feel an ineffable well-being when you were able to vent to a person in your confidence the anguish that was going through your heart?
>
> ...
>
> Of course, it is not enough to empty the spirit. When it's empty, something has to enter it. The spirit cannot stay long in a vacuum. One cannot stay permanently with it empty'. I admit that there may be people capable of accomplishing such a feat. Gradually, it is necessary to 'fill it' again, otherwise those old unpleasant thoughts, which had been hurled away, will seek to return again.
>
> To prevent this from happening, start quickly to fill the spirit with creative and healthy

thoughts. So when the old fears, hatreds, and tribulations that beset you for so long seek to settle back into your spirit, you will find a sign on the door that says, busy.'

Do not allow occasional thoughts of doubt and skepticism to take root in your mind. Counteract this, at once, the biblical passages containing the divine promises, which every Christian must have stored in memory.

Never be overwhelmed by the language of worldly unbelief. The world centers its security on the things of the world and considers man self-sufficient, while the Christian rests his trust in God.

To give life to Deusconstitui, essentially, an act of faith. It is an act of dispossession. [432]

When one feeds one's inner self with evil designs, it will defile our whole being and we cannot please God.

To seek God is also to preserve our mind and our heart from those old thoughts and feelings that made us slaves of sin, because, in the words of the Lord Jesus, our eyes are the lamp of the body. We must always seek the renewal of mind and heart by daily communion with God, through prayer and the reading of the Bible. [433]

It is very important, in this process, that we know how to choose what to read (books, internet, *newspapers*, magazines) and watch (television, internet). Temptations will certainly arise, but we need not succumb to them, because no one is tempted beyond their strength. We can't stop birds from flying above our heads, but we can stop them from nesting on our heads.

Our soul is nourished with Biblical promises and truths. There is nothing more powerful than the biblical words associated with the faith of the one who meditates them and keeps them in his heart. God acts from the faith of the person, not a generic belief, but a specific faith founded on the Word of God. It is through this specific faith that miracles and the working of God take place in the lives of believers.

Try to read the Bible and mark the passages that contain promises, positive and comforting ideas, and passages that relate to faith. You will be amazed at the richness of the stimulating messages that God's Word holds for each of us.

6.6 *Sharing*

The sharing of the good news translates the noblest form of love to the neighbor, because in this way, we will demonstrate that we are truly interested in the fate of our fellow man.

Jesus emphasized the divine role in sharing, by associating the faithful with the light and salt of the world.

It is up to the believer to share the Bread of Life with which he was given, for it reveals how much we care about the life of our neighbour.

Jesus left us the parable of the silver coins:[434]

> "A high-born man traveled to a far-off region to invest himself as king and returned called ten of his servants, distributed among them ten coins of great value, and said to them, «Negotiate until I return. 'But his fellow citizens hated him and sent a delegation after him to say 'We do not want him to reign over us'. And when he was come again invested as king, he commanded to call the servants before him, to whom he had distributed the money, to know what business every man had done. The first came and said: «Lord, your coin has yielded ten coins. ' He said to him: Very well, good servant! For thou hast been faithful in a little matter, receive thou authority over ten cities. The

second came and said, Thy coin, O Lord, hath brought forth five coins. 'He said likewise to this: 'As for you, take the direction of five cities. 'Another came and said, 'Lord, behold your coin, which I had put aside in a cloth. I was afraid of you, because you are a severe man: you take what you did not put and reap where you did not sow. 'He said to him, 'According to your own words, evil servant, I will judge you. You knew I'm a strict man, that I take what I haven't deposited and reap where I haven't sown. Then why didn't you deposit my money in the bank? When I returned, I would have recovered it with interest. 'Then, I said to those who were there: «Take your coin and give it to the ten'. They said to him, 'Lord, he already has ten pieces' - I tell you, every man who has will be given; but to him who has not, even what he has will be taken away. As for my enemies, those who did not want me to reign over them, bring them here and kill them in my presence." em seguida. Ele

Jesus wants us to see our neighbor as Christ Himself as He teaches in Matthew 25:40 and 45, with whom we must first share the heavenly bread without forgetting the material needs of our neighbor.

The light of Jesus that is in the Christian should be distributed as the next, for He taught us that the lamp should be placed in the proper place, and not under the bed, so that the whole room may be illuminated, according to Mark 21.

6.7 *Consecrating*

To consecrate a priest to the Lord in Hebrew means "to fill his hands" with offerings. At the time of the First Covenant, when the priest was offering burnt offerings, he was consecrated to the Lord. [435]

God had appointed Aaron - Moses' brother - as priest and Aaron's grandson, Pine-tree, as perpetual priest. Pines killed a Medianite and the Israelite who brought her to the camp, to prevent the Lord God from exterminating the Israelites because they had prostituted themselves with the daughters of Moab and worshipped their gods. [436]

To assist the Priests, God separated for himself the members of the tribe of Levi, who were descendants of Aaron (who also came from Levi). Thus, the Levites had no military obligations and were not recorded for this purpose (Numbers 1:47). The Levites were placed at the disposal of the priests, at their service and at the service of the whole community in front of the Tent of Meeting, to secure the office of the dwelling, and they were also to watch over the utensils of the House of God (Numbers 3:5 to 8).

The Levites were also consecrated to the LORD according to Numbers 8.

Priests wore special garments and had to follow certain rituals. Only the High Priest could enter the Most Holy Place of the Tabernacle, transposing the veil that separated him from the rest of the Temple. Any other Jew who entered this Holy Place was struck down immediately.

The death of the Messiah caused the veil of the Tabernacle to be torn from top to bottom, allowing the Holy Spirit to inhabit the body of Christians and convict the world of sin and judgment.

By the Old Covenant, only priests were consecrated. From Jesus, it is all Christians who are called and chosen for the service of God. This is not an exclusivity of either Christian, but of all Christianity.

Being at the service of God is not only an assignment of ministers of the faith, such as pastors and missionaries. All who have accepted Jesus as their teacher and savior are enabled to participate in the work of God.

The service of God is not a burden to be borne, but is a privilege that distinguishes every Son from God. Divine grace gives us all the tools for the work. The work is of God, but He gives us the privilege of being co-partners, placing us in His hands, so that the work may be accomplished.

It is the Lord God who gives us love, joy and all qualities so that we may love him, as well as our neighbour. It is the Holy Spirit who convicts not only dwarves but the world of sin and the final judgment. It is enough for the believer to share Jesus with his neighbor, that the Lord God will work in his life.

Working in the harvest of God we are only returning a small part of what He has given us.

What services can be offered to God? They are the most varied. Within your community, you'll find a job. It can be welcoming the brothers in the cult, participating in the choir, playing a musical instrument, integrating prayer and praise groups, participating in the administration of the community, working with children, young or old etc.

In my case, I chose to write books telling my experience with God. I think right now it's the best way to contribute to the Kingdom of God.

Jesus went deeper into the subject and taught that it is up to us to visit sick and imprisoned; feed and clothe the little brethren who are in need.[437]

Walking with Jesus is recognizing your leadership over our lives. When Jesus called Nathanael a true Israelite and told him that he had seen him the day before - in spirit - under the fig tree, he called Jesus Rabbi, Savior and King of Israel.[438]

The vast majority of people throughout the world recognize Jesus as a teacher, as a being versed in religion or philosophy. These people consider Jesus on the same level as great thinkers, such as Buddha, Confucius, Socrates and others.

Another smaller portion of the world sees Jesus **only** as Savior; They have accommodated themselves in their search for God and seek to deceive themselves that they are attending the ordinances of God with this superficial conviction.

Finally, an even smaller portion of the world's population regards Jesus Christ as their King and Messiah. Its components are ready to obey Christ as the Master of their lives, stripping themselves of their selfish and sinful desires, or, as in the words of Jesus, denying themselves. Their lives and possessions are consecrated to the service of their King in a constant quest for sanctification. They are ready to obey Christ and are willing to deny themselves and carry their cross. They are willing to let go of everything, if necessary, to follow Jesus Christ.

As long as you are seeking Jesus only as a wise man and as the savior of mankind, you will not find him. You will be seeking only personal benefit, regardless of the mission of evangelization, solidarity or the fruits of Christian life. You will be selfish and will continue to cling to your material and carnal concerns.

The moment you sincerely wish to give up your life of sin and long for the Messiah to take up residence in your life, then, yes, things will begin to happen.

Paul writes, "Know ye not that ye are the temple of God, and that the Spirit of God dwelleth in you? If anyone destroys the temple of God, God will destroy him. For the temple of God is holy, and that temple is you".[439]

Our body, therefore, is the temple of God, as had been the tabernacle in relation to the times of the first covenant. Sin is a desecration of the place where God dwells.

The Christians of the early church sold everything they owned and deposited at the feet of the Apostles, who distributed their goods and their profit according to the needs of each one.

This model has lost strength and today Christian communities depend on the contributions and tithes of their control of the Heavenly Council, formed by Yahweh, the Holy Spirit and Jesus of Nazareth. Consider that you as well as everything you have belongs to you - on loan from the Creator - and put everything at your disposal to be used in the way that suits the Kingdom. members. This does not prevent you from consecrating yourself and your possessions entirely to the

Jesus consecrated his whole life to the will of the Father, culminating in surrendering his own life to save many. Many Christians, as history tells us, have already lost their lives because they are intransigent with their convictions. The time is approaching when there will be persecution of all who truly profess Christ, beginning a period of death, both spiritual, physical and economic.

There can be no greater proof of consecration to God than to be willing to die for Christ's sake. This is the kind of worshiper God seeks: he has his eyes toward eternity; is convinced that life - here on earth - is only a transitory passage and that an endless life awaits you in the glorious company of God. The apostle Paul argues that it was better for him to die and be with God eternally than to live transiently enduring suffering.

When we have eyes toward eternity, we no longer give importance to fears and are no longer guided by them; We are convinced that we are of God and He will quicken us. The other lesser fears also fade away in the certainty that we will have a wonderful and indescribable life in the heavenly spheres.

We can hardly find a degree of consecration as demonstrated by Abraham, the father of the Jews and the Arabs.

Let us remember that he, being of a very advanced age, was blessed by God and begat a son named Isaac. God wanted to test Abraham's self-denial and ordered him to offer his own son as a burnt offering, the one who would be the father of the Jews and Arabs and with whom God had promised to establish a "perpetual covenant, to be his God and that of his race after him".[440][441]

Imagine this situation: God had commanded Abraham to exterminate the person he loved most in this world, his own son. Abraham obeyed God and was ready to strike a death blow to Isaac on Mount Moriah, when God stopped him and provided him with a little lamb to be slain.[442]

Perhaps Abraham suspected that God was testing him. Facing Isaac's perplexity over the lack of an animal for the burnt offering, Abraham replied, "God will provide".[443]

How many times in our lives can we say, with Abraham, "God will provide"? How often are we willing to give up everything for the Gospel?

When seeking God, another faith that is not in accordance with the divine plan is faith centered on itself.

When we accept Jesus Christ, we often interpret, or are led to interpret, that our "I" is situated at the center of God's will.

There is no doubt that the human being is loved immensely by God, so much so that his Son emptied himself of his dependents. . to suffer and die so that many might be saved. But God did not cease to be God and our creator, nor we to be creatures and beings

The self-centered Christian's biblical reading is subverting the biblical order of how to seek God. First, we must seek the Kingdom of God, and secondly, God will add all the necessary things. This is what Master Jesus taught: "Seek ye first the kingdom of God, and his righteousness; and all these things shall be added unto you." (Matthew 6:33-34) Jesus referred to the disciples' food and clothing when he mentioned "all these things".

There is no biblical support for the idea that Jesus came to make Christians prosperous. Jesus taught that we should not worry about what we should wear or eat, because God will provide these basic needs while they are working on the Kingdom mission. The biblical order is this: first the Kingdom of God; then the satisfaction of personal needs. We must take care not to reverse these values and put our personal life plans into , or seek only the blessings and not the winner of them. top of our prayers

The Word of God is timeless, it is destined for today, as it will be destined for the distant tomorrow, as it was already turned to the past. The Word of God does not change according to contingencies or political and social circumstances. Contingencies can alter the way the word is accepted and assimilated, but they do not produce any change in God's response, that is, the divine promises are the same yesterday, today and forever.

In our prayers, it is common to concern ourselves with our personal needs, and we put the attainment of God's will in the background. God does his will with the concurrence of human participation. And this participation also occurs through prayer. Just as God made use of His Word to accomplish creation and to sustain life, He allows us, in His likeness, also to manifest Himself by word and to be co-participants in the accomplishment of His will. In the Our

Father's prayer, Jesus teaches us to ask that "the divine will be done" "on earth as it is in heaven".

Consecrated prayer is that which has as its main objective the divine will. The will of God is that the whole world be evangelized and as many people as possible attain salvation. We can pray for the advancement of Christianity and conversion of those close to us, including our enemies; the success of evangelistic and missionary campaigns throughout the world, including in Israel and the Arab countries; by the workings of Satan; so that the time of the antichrist may be shortened; that the church of Christ may be enlarged both in number and in quality; that God may raise up more workers to serve in His harvest in all jobs and fronts of work; by Christians who are being persecuted all over the world and by the inoperative forces of evil upon them.

The will of God is also that we have well-being. But when we pray for the fulfillment of our personal needs, we must want the fulfillment of those needs to enable us to be instruments of God for the fulfillment of His purposes. The well-being of our prayers will always be a secondary goal, while the primary request should always be the attainment of God's will. In this way, we will not make the mistake of saying superficial prayers that seek only personal benefits.

Watchman Nee discusses the subject: "When we pray, we naturally do it for our own well-being. We have needs, desires and expectations and then we pray for them. We pray to supply our requests. Even so, in true prayer we should not simply ask for the things related to our own well-being, we should also pray for the glory of God and for heaven to rule the earth. Answer to prayer gives the Lord much glory, for it reveals the excellent greatness of his love and power in attending to the request of his children".[444]

One of Jesus' great teachings is that we should pray for God to raise up workers to his harvest. Said Jesus: "the harvest is great, but the workers are small. Ask therefore the Lord of the harvest to send out laborers for his harvest"[445]

Many people believe that living with God is being immune to suffering. What God promises is that He will be with us at all times, even when we are crossing the valley of the shadow of death (Psalm 23). But the Bible does not say that we will not cross the valley of the shadow of death; The Bible doesn't say we won't suffer. The Lord Jesus called Paul to the ministry telling him that he would have to suffer exceedingly in his name.   Throughout history, Christians have been persecuted and there have been many divisions between them. Jesus said he did not come to bring peace to the world, for he knew that his message would bring discord even among family members.[446]

6.8 *Persevering*

Seeking God is not only the formula of one who seeks a first real experience with Christ. Those who find it find an incomparable treasure and it is wise to want to preserve this communion. The formula of communion is to seek God always!

We must remember that the attainment of redemption involves perseverance, because our passage on earth is relatively enduring, and throughout the journey we must always seek God's presence in our lives. Jesus teaches us that salvation is maintained at the expense of perseverance.[447]

So we can understand why Jesus said that He is the way.[448] It is as if we were participating in a marathon, for which it was not so important to cross the finish line, but to win each of those that separate us from that finish line. We are athletes of Christ and the purpose of each one is to preserve his incorruptible crown (salvation) until the end of the race. 42 quilômetros[449]

When our sins are remitted and we are sanctified, we must seek to preserve our new nature in Christ and consequently our sanctification, by turning away from all that can lead us to the return of the practice of sin and continually seek the presence of God. The part that belongs to us in the process of sanctification is to go **to God, turning away** from all evil.

We will be abusing grace when we intentionally return to the practice of a sin already forgiven, assuming that God will continue to forgive us forever.

Surely whoever abides in Christ to the end will receive the incorruptible crown:

> "Whosoever the Father giveth me shall come to me, and whosoever cometh to me I will not cast him away: for I came not down from heaven to do my will, but the will of him that sent me. And this is the will of him that sent me, that I should

lose nothing that he gave me, but should raise it up at the last day. Yes, this is the will of my Father: whoever sees the Son and believes in him has eternal life, and I will raise him up at the last day."[450]

May God help us to persevere to the end of our days here on earth.

7 *Bibliographic References*

Diverse translators. 10. ed. São Paulo: Editora Mundo Cristão, 1997.

The Bible of Jerusalem. Several translators. São Paulo: Pauline Editions, 1981.

The New Life Bible. Translated by João Ferreira de Almeida. 2. ed. São Paulo: S.R. Edições Vida Nova, 1978.

Bible Studies New International Version. Editora Vida, 2003.

Bible Ecumenical Translation. Editions Loyola, 1994.

BERKOUWER, G.C. *Biblical Doctrine of Sin.* São Paulo: Editora Aste, 1970.

CHESNOFF, Richard Z. *Bando de Ladrões. 1.* ed. São Paulo: Editora Manole, 2001.

DANTAS. *Programa de Direito Civil.* 4. ed.4. issue Editora Rio.

FLUSSER. *Jesus.* Editora Perspectiva, 2002.

MIEN, Aleksandr. *Jesus Master of Nazareth.* New Town Publishing House, 2002.

MORIN, Emile. *Jesus and the Structures of His Time.* São Paulo: Pauline Editions, 1981.

NEE, Watchman. *The Normal Christian Life.* São Paulo: Editora Fiel Ltda., 1979.

ORTIZ, Juan Carlos. The disciple. Minas Gerais: Editora Betânia, 1978.

PEALE, this is Norman Vincent. *The Power of Positive Thinking.* Editora Cultrix.

SANDERS, J. Oswald. *Paul the Leader.* Editora Vida, 1986.

SCHLESINGER, Hugo. *Jesus was a Jew.* Hugo Schlesinger, Humberto Porto. São Paulo: Pauline Editions, 1979.

WARREN, Rick. *A Life with Purposes.* Editora Vida, 2003.

---

[1] The Biblical transcripts, when not indicated by source, were taken from the Jerusalem Bible.

2   "26. God said, Let us make man in our image and likeness, and let them rule over the fish of the sea, and the fowl of the air, and the cattle, and all the beasts, and every creeping thing that creepeth upon the earth. '27. God created man in his own image, in the image of God created him, man and woman created he them."

3   In Genesis 2, we read: "4-b. In time he made the earth and the heaven, ... 7. Then Iahweh God modeled man with the clay of the soil, inflated his nostrils em que Iahweh Deusa breath of life and man became a living being." The breath of life (neshamá) gave rise to the soul (néfesh) and the spirit (Ruah), attributes that make the human being similar to the Most High (cf. Genesis 1:26 and 27).

4 Genesis 1: "God said, Let us make man in our image, after our likeness, and let him subject the fish of the sea, the birds of the sky, the great beasts, the whole earth, and all the little beasts that creep upon the earth! '"

5 Cf. Luke 12:24.

6 "... If the dead do not rise, let us eat and drink, for tomorrow we die."

7 Cf. Genesis 6:3.

8   Paul probably combines Isaiah 64:3 with Jeremiah 3:16. In Isaiah 64:3, we read, "From ancient times it was never heard, it was never known, the eye had not seen a God acting for those who wait for him, except for you." In Jeremiah 3:16, we read, "When ye shall multiply and be fruitful in the earth, in those days - the oracle of Yahweh - it shall be no more

said: 'The ark of the covenant of Yaweh'; She shall not return to memory, they shall remember her no more, they shall not seek her, nor be rebuilt."

9   "45. The kingdom of heaven is like unto a merchant seeking fine pearls. 46. When he finds a pearl of great price, he goes and sells all that he has and buys."

10   Ephesians 2:8: "For by grace you are saved through faith; And it's not up to you, it's God's gift. This doesn't come from the works for anyone to be proud of."

11   Revelation 3: "14. To the Angel of the Church in Laodicea, write: Thus speaks the Amen, the faithful and true Witness, the Beginning of God's creation, 15. I know your conduct: you are neither cold nor hot. I wish you were cold or hot! 16. So because you are warm, neither cold nor hot, I vomit you out of my mouth."

12   Such as, for example, the parable of the rich man (Luke 12:16-21), the parable of the ten virgins (Matthew 25:3) and the parable of the servants awaiting the return of their Lord (Luke 12:35-40).

13   "Of that day and that hour knoweth no man, no, not the angels of heaven, nor the Son, but only the Father."

14   In December 2004, there was a tsunami (*tsunami*), which devastated 8 Asian countries and killed more than 150,000 people directly.

15   He was sitting on the Mount of Olives, when the disciples approached him alone and said, "Tell us when this is going to be, and what is the sign of your coming and of the end of time." 4. Jesus replied, "Beware lest anyone deceive you. 5. For many will come in my name, saying, 'I am the Messiah', and will deceive many. 6. You will hear of wars and rumors of

war. Be careful not to be alarmed. It must happen, but it is not yet the end. 7. For nation will rise against nation and kingdom against kingdom. And there will be famine and earthquakes everywhere. All this will be the beginning of pain. At that time they shall deliver you up to tribulation, and slay you, and ye shall be hated of all people for my name's sake. 10. And then many will be scandalized and give themselves to each other and hate each other. 11. And false prophets shall rise in great numbers, and shall deceive many. 12 And by the increase of iniquity the love of many shall wax cold. 13. But he that endureth to the end, the same shall be saved. 14. And this Gospel of the kingdom shall be proclaimed throughout the whole world as a testimony to all nations. And then comes the End."

[16] Judaism accepts only the Old Testament and Orthodox Jews are awaiting the first coming of the Messiah.

[17] The figures were drawn, by rounding, from the Encyclopedia Barsa, v. 7, 1979.

[18] *Inbandodeladrões, Editora* Manole, 1999, p. 19-20.

[19] Cf. Matthew 12:37.

[20] Jesus was amazed at the faith professed by a Roman centurion and therefore by a Gentile (not a Jew). This is what is read in Matthew 8:10: "10. When Jesus heard this, he was astonished, and said unto them that followed him, Verily I say unto you, In Israel have I found none such faith. But I say unto you, That there shall come many from the east of the west, and shall sit down in the kingdom of heaven with Abraham, Isaac, and Jacob, while the children of the kingdom shall be set out in darkness, where there shall be weeping and gnashing of teeth. '"

21   According to Berkouwer (b. cit., p. 17), the Bible does not deal with explaining the first cause of sin, which is one of the mysteries of faith, but indicates the confession of guilt as accepting its responsibility.

22   "19. For what may be known of God is manifest among them, for God has revealed it to them. 20. His invisible reality - his eternal power and divinity - has become intelligible, since the creation of the world, through creatures, so that they have no excuse. 21. For when they knew God, they honoured him not as God, neither yielded thanks unto him; On the contrary, they lost them in vain arrayed and their foolish heart stood in darkness."

23   Isaiah 59:1. "No, Yahweh's hand is not too short to save, nor his ear so hard that he cannot hear. 2. But it is your iniquities that have created an abyss between you and your God. For your sins he hid his face from you, that he might not hear you. 3. Your hands are stained with blood, and your fingers with iniquity; Your lips speak lies, and your tongue speaketh wickedness."

Psalm 5. "5. You are not a God who loves wickedness, the wicked are not your guest. 6. No, the arrogant do not remain in your presence. You hate all evildoers. 7. You destroy liars, the bloodthirsty and deceitful man Iahweh rejects him."

24   Romans 6:6 (New Life Bible version: "Knowing this, that our old man was crucified with him, that the body of sin might be destroyed, and that we should not serve sin as slaves."

25   An expression probably coined by Paul, which corresponds to the "new birth in the Spirit" referred to by Jesus (John 3:3).

This aspect is best developed in the chapter "Sanctifying Oneself".
According to Romans 6: "6. Let us understand this well: our old man was
crucified with him, so that this body of sin may be destroyed, and so that
we may no longer be slaves to sin" and cf. Colossians 3: "9. Let there be no
more lies among you, for you have divested the old man, with his practices,
and clothed the new man, who, to gain access to knowledge, never ceases
to be renewed in the image of his Creator." Both citations were extracted
from BTE.

26   Christianity provoked a real revolution in the
"humanization" of the world in interpersonal relations and these with the
authorities. The reader can imagine the barbarism that would be the world
without the Christian principles that are taught from an early age.

27   That is, in the world of facts, where attitudes can be
apprehended through the five senses. The spiritual world concerns the
"inner man", his values and his mind.

28   Together with this, it should be borne in mind that sin
transcends mere relations of human coexistence, placing itself in the direct
link between God and man, as, p. g. The first three commandments of
Exodus 20. Note that sin is an appreciation that God makes and its
conformation is independent of there being an appreciable "humanly"
harm (e.g. two people are in sin without there being any harm in their
appreciation). However, in the example cited and within the spiritual
dimension, this damage exists and its consequence is the absence or break
of communion with God. It should be noted that even sins regarded as of
human coexistence were probably established in direct function of God's

appreciation of justice and faithfulness; that is, they are, first and foremost, an attack on the loving desire for communion with God. As God the Son taught, there is no truth in saying that we love God, whom we do not see, if we stop loving our neighbor, who is at our side.

[29]   Cf. Psalm 94:11: "Iahweh knows the thoughts of man, yes, and they are but a breath." Other references can be found in Job 21:27, Psalm 56:5, Psalm 139:2, Psalm 139:23, and Isaiah 59:7.

[30]   Cf. Romans 3:23.

[31]   Matthew 23: "27. Woe to you, scribes and Pharisees, hypocrites! You are like whitewashed tombs, which on the outside look beautiful, but on the inside are full of dead bones and all filth. 28. Even so you also: outwardly you appear righteous to men, but inwardly you are full of hypocrisy and iniquity."

[32]   Psalms 5: "9. Guide me with your righteousness, Iahweh, because of those who besiege me. Make straight your way before me! 10. For there is no sincerity in your mouth, your heart is full of machinations; His throat is an open sepulchre and his tongue is fluent."

[33]   "We know that the law is spiritual, but I am carnal, sold as a slave to sin. I really can't understand what I'm doing; For I do not practice what I will, but do what I hate. Now, if I do what I don't want to do, I recognize that the law is good. In fact, it is no longer I who do the deed, but the sin that dwells I know that good does not dwell in me, that is, in my flesh. For the will of the good is within my power, but not the doing of it. In fact, I do not do the good that I want, but I do the evil that I do not want. Now if I do that which I would not, it is no longer I that act, but sin that

dwelleth in me. And I perceive this law, that when I will do good, evil bringeth it unto me. I delight in the law of God according to the inward man, but I perceive another law in my members, which warreth against the law of my reason, and bindeth me to the law of sin which is in my members." (Romans em mim. Eu7:13-23)

34   Our body, considered in itself, is not unclean. The Son of God Himself became flesh and dwelt among us, but He did not commit any sin.

35 *Inuma Vida com Propósito, Editora* Vida, p. 19.

36   Ob. cit. , p. 18.

37   Matthew 5: "29. If your right eye causes you to sin, pluck it out and throw it away from you, for it is better that one of your limbs be lost than that your whole body be cast into Geena. 30. If thy right *hand* cause thee to sin, cut it off, and cast it far from thee: for it is better for one of thy members to perish, than for thy whole body to go into the garden."

38   Matthew 10: "28. Do not be afraid of those who kill the body, but cannot kill the soul. Rather fear the one who can destroy the soul and the body in the *Geena*."

39   Ephesians 2:19-21: "So you are no longer foreigners or migrants; You are fellow citizens of the saints, you are of the family of God. You have been integrated into the foundation of the apostles and prophets, and Jesus Christ Himself as the foundation stone. It is in him that every building sets and rises to form a holy temple in the Lord."

40   1st Peter 2:11: "The Christian existence among the heathen. Dear friends! I exhort you, as strangers and pilgrims, to abstain from fleshly lusts, which war against the soul."

41   1st John 5:19: "We know that we are of God and that the whole world is under the power of the evil one."

42   "A good man out of the good treasure of his heart bringeth forth that which is good: but an evil man bringeth forth that which is evil out of his evil: For the mouth speaks of that whereof the heart is full." (Matthew 12:35)

43   Cf. Luke 11:34 to 36.

44   Cf.Philippians 4:8.

45   John 14: "30. I will no longer tell you much, for the prince of the world comes; Against me he can do nothing, but the world will know that I love the Father and do as the Father has commanded me." John 12: "It is now the judgment of this world, now the prince of this world will be cast out; And when I am lifted up from the earth, I will draw all to myself."

46   All the angels of God have light and receive it from God, who is Light. The name Lucifer emphasizes the special intensity of light and celestial hierarchy. With the downfall, Lucifer lost the heavenly light and he is now the prince of darkness.

47   Isaiah 14:12-15 in the New Life version of the Bible.

48   "For our struggle is not against blood nor against the flesh, but against the principalities, against the Authorities, against the Rulers of this dark world, against the Spirits of Evil, who populate the heavenly regions."

49   Mark 9. 28: "When he went into the house, his disciples asked him alone, 'Why could we not cast him out'? 29. He answered, «This kind cannot come out except by prayer. '"

50   We are not addressing the time of apostasy in which believers will die to preserve their faith: the name of Jesus will gradually be prohibited from being pronounced (attack on sharing) and from being mentalized (attack on spiritual edification). This period will correspond to the "yellow or greenish horse" of which the Apocalypse speaks (6:7), and will be characterized by the relentless persecution of Christians. This apocalyptic passage is in keeping with the prophecy about the beast and his prophet (Revelation 13:16-17), when only those who worship the beast or bear his name may buy or sell, whereas those who refuse this will have decreed their economic and/or physical death. Notice that we are living the time that the Bible calls "black horse", which is characterized by a period of predominance of justice and its popularization, which succeeded the "red horse", which symbolized the great world wars. Each of these periods has a prevalent tonic, but its characteristics are interwoven.

51   "You belong to the devil, your father, and you want to fulfill your father's wishes. He was a murderer from the beginning, because there is no truth in him: when he lies, he speaks his own things, because he is a liar and the father of lies."

52 1st John 5:19: "We know that we are of God, but the whole world lies in the power of the evil one." (BTE version)

53   "And it's no surprise! For Satan himself is transfigured into an angel of light."

54   *See* Matthew 24:24.

55   Isaiah 55. "11. So it also happens with the word that comes out of my mouth: it will not return to me empty, but will do what I desire and achieve the purpose for which I sent it." (Bible version of NIV study)

56   Galatians 5: "1. It is to be truly free that Christ has made us free. Stand firm, therefore, and do not allow yourselves to be subjected again to the yoke of slavery." (Bible version, ecumenical translation)

57   I John 1: "9. If we claim to be sinless, deceive ourselves, and the truth is not confessing our sins, he is faithful and just to forgive our sins and cleanse us from all unrighteousness. If we claim that we have not committed sin, we make God a liar, and His word is not in us." (NIV Study Bible version)em nós. Se

58   The institutions are the varied denominations created by man, seen by their structural, financial and legal aspects. Throughout history, these institutions have often bowed to secular power. The invisible church has Christ as its head and believers as its independently denominational branches.

59   *See* commentary at the end of this chapter on the abomination of desolation.

60   Satan himself was once an angel endowed with great light, hence the origin of his former name (Lucifer). But this light did not come from himself, but from God, and could not accompany him after the expulsion from heaven. But Satan "disguises himself as an angel of light" and his followers as "servants of righteousness" (BTE, 2 Corinthians 11:14-15).

61   Cf. 1 [John 5]:18.

62   Revelation 13: "14. Thanks to the wonders granted to her to perform the service of the Beast, she seduces the inhabitants of the earth, urging them to make an image in honor of the Beast who had been wounded by the sword, but returned to life. 15. He was even given to infuse spirit into the image of the Beast, so that the image could speak and cause all who did not worship the image of the Beast to die. 16. And he caused all, both small and great, rich and poor, free and bond, to receive a mark in their hand, or in their foreheads, 17. so that no one can buy or sell without the mark, the name of the Beast or the number of his name. 18. Here discernment is needed! Whoever is intelligent calculate the number of the Beast, for it is a man's number: his number is 666!"

63   Cf. Mark 13:14; 19-20.

64   According to, for example, Daniel 2:44: "In the time of these kings, the God of heaven will establish a kingdom that will never be destroyed and that will never be dominated by any other people. He will destroy all the kingdoms of those kings and exterminate them, but that kingdom will last forever." (NIV Study Bible)

[65]This is a matter of torment, of abstracting the first cause of the concausas that originate the sinful act.

66   *Biblical Doctrine of Sin, p.* 13.

67   Psalm 23: "1. Iahweh is my shepherd, I lack nothing. He maketh me to lie down in green pastures. He leadeth me unto still waters, and restoreth my strength: He leadeth me in the paths of righteousness for

his name's sake. 4. Though I walk through a valley of darkness, I will fear no evil: for thy rod and thy staff are with me, they leave me at ease... 6. Yea, happiness and love shall follow me all the days of my life: My address is Iahweh's house for days on end."

Psalm 119:68: "You are good and good, teach me your statutes."

[68]   Psalm 27: "1. Iahweh is my light and my salvation: of whom shall I be afraid? Iahweh is the fortress of my life: before whom will I tremble?"

[69]   Job 34: "10. Listen to me, wise men. Far from God the evil, from Shaddai, the iniquity!" "12. In fact, God does not do evil, Shaddai does not pervert the right."

[70]   Job 34: "11. He rewards a man according to his works, and gives to every man according to his manner." Psalm 73: "27. Yes, those who turn away from you are lost, you repel all your adulterers. 28. As for me, being with God is my good! In God I put my shelter, to count all your works."

[71]   Ob. cit., p. 12.

[72]   Genesis 1:31: "God saw all that He had done: and it was very good..."

[73]   Genesis 2: "7. Then Yahweh modeled man with the clay of the ground, and breathed into his nostrils a breath of life, and man became a living being."

[74]   Genesis 2:24: "Therefore a man leaves his father and mother, and joins his wife, and they become one flesh."

[75]   Including and especially the bodies of the First Couple, since there was no malice.

[76]   Pride in its exponential manifestation lies in the human desire to be "god", to judge and condemn one's fellow man by his own will and convenience.

[77]   Ob. cit. , p. 22.

[78]   Ob. cit. , pp. 77 and 78.

[79]   Luther's position, which we support, is that there was no free will for man. He was forbidden to eat from a certain tree and disobeyed this precept. The argument seems to be definitive to dismiss any excuse of the First Couple.

[80]   Genesis 22:1-2: "Now after these events God put Abraham to the test and said to him, 'O Abraham,' he answered, 'Behold,

Here I am. He continued: take your son, your only son, Isaac, whom you love. Go into the land of Moriah, and offer it there for a burnt offering upon one of the mountains which I show thee. '"

[81]   BTE, Exodus 16: "The Lord said to Moses, I will cause bread to rain from heaven for you. The people must go out to gather the daily ration every day, so that I may put it to the test: will it walk or not in my law? '"

[82]   Book of Sirach, chapter 15, verse 20, final part, BTE.

[83]   Book of Sirach, chapter 15, verse 14, final part, BTE.

[84]   Expression contained in the Hebrew Bible as commentary to the book of Sirach 14:14, letter "m".

[85]   At this point, the association with the contract seems more distant. In times of full justice, no contract can enslave man.

----

86 Deuteronomy 32: "3. I will proclaim the name of Iahweh; As for you, magnify our God! 4. He is the Rock, and his work is perfect; for all his conduct is the Law. He is true God and without injustice, he himself is Justice and Righteousness." Also in Isaiah 14:12 to 15 in the New Life version of the Bible.

87   Genesis 17: "1. When Abram was ninety years old, Yahweh appeared to him and said to him: «I am El Shadddai, walk in my presence and be perfect. 2. I declare my covenant between me and you, and I will multiply you exceedingly. ' 3. And Abram fell on his face. God8. A spoke thus to him: 4. As for me, behold my covenant with thee: thou shalt be the father of a multitude of nations. 5. And thy name shall be called no more Abram: but thy name shall be Abraham: for I have made thee the father of a multitude of nations. 6. I will make thee exceedingly fruitful, I will make nations of thee, and kings shall come out of thee. 7. I will establish my covenant between me and you, and your race after you, from generation to generation, an everlasting covenant, to be your God, and that of your race after you. You, and your race after you, I will give the land in which you live, the whole land of Canaan, for an everlasting possession, and I will be your God... 10. And behold my covenant, which shall be observed between me and you, that is, your race after you, that all your males be circumcised...' 15. And God said unto Abraham, I pray thee, Sarai thy wife shall call her no more; but her name is Sarah. 16. I will bless her, and give thee a son therefrom: I will bless her, she shall become nations, and out of them shall come kings of peoples. '"

88   Circumcision is the surgery that cuts the glans covering the penis (foreskin).

89   Cf. Genesis 17:15-27.

90   Isaac's son, Jacob, came to a fight with the angel of God, which is why he was called Israel (Genesis 35:10). Their offspring gave rise to the 12 tribes of Israel. The sons of Israel, according to Genesis 35:22 to 26, were the following: Havidos of Leah, Reuben, Simeon, Levi, Judah, Issachar, and Zabulon; The words of Rachel, Joseph, and Benjamin, The servants of Bala, Rachel, Dan, and Nephtali; Zelfa, the handmaid of Leah, Gad, and Asher.

91 Genesis 41:39. "Since God has made all this known to you, there is none so intelligent and wise as you. 40. Thou shalt be the steward of my palace, and all my people shall obey thy charge; only in the throne shall I precede thee.".

92   "The Lord said to Moses, Behold, you shall sleep with your fathers; And this people shall begin to commit fornication after the gods of the strangers, which are in the land, whither he goeth in; He will forsake me, break my covenant that I have established with him. '" (Deuteronomy 31:16)

93   According to the note "a" to verse 14 of Exodus 3, BTE; and according to Aleksandr Mien, in "Jesus Master of Nazareth", p. 25.

94   Cf. Exodus 3:14, BTE.

95   Ob. cit. , p. 24.

96   According to several biblical passages in the translation of John Ferreira de Almeida and the Jerusalem Bible (Iahweh dos Exércitos): 1

Samuel 17:45; 1 Chronicles 11:9; 1 Chronicles 17:24; Isaiah 6:3, 8:13 and 14:27. The BTE prefers to use, unchanged in meaning, other expressions, as in the text of 1 Samuel 17:45: "David said to the Philistine, Thou comest against me armed with sword, spear, and javelin; But I come unto thee armed with sword, and with spear, and with javelin; But I come unto thee armed with the name of the LORD of all power, the God of the ranks of Israel, whom thou hast defied. '"

[97]   Cf. note "b" to verse 15 of Exodus 3.

[98]   "Standing in the middle of the areopagus, Paul spoke: «Athenians, I consider, in every respect, men almost too religious. In fact, when I walk through your streets, my gaze is often turned to your sacred monuments, and I have discovered, among others, an altar with this inscription: «To the unknown god'. What you venerate in this way, without knowing it, is what I have come to announce to you. '" (Acts 17:22 to 23, BTE)

[99]   Cf.Matthew 6:24.

[100]   "Jesus said unto his disciples, This is why I say unto you, Take no thought for your life, what ye shall eat, nor for your body, what ye shall wear. For life is more than food and the body, more than clothing. '" (Luke 12:22-23)

[101]   Matthew 19: "22. And Jesus said to his disciples, Verily, I say to you, a rich man will hardly enter the kingdom of heaven. 23. I repeat, it is easier for a camel to pass through the eye of a needle than for a rich man to enter the Kingdom of God. ' 25. Before these words the disciples were greatly impressed and said: «Who then can be saved? 'Gazing

at them, Jesus said to them: 'To men it is impossible, but to God everything is possible. '" The BTE brings the following comment: "And. Probably alluding to the tiny eye of a sewing needle, not to a low-walled city door. It is a hyperbola of a very oriental nature, which must be interpreted in its context."

[102] According to Luke: "But woe unto you, ye rich men, ye have your consolation." (verse 24, BTE)

[103] Acts 4:32 to 35: "The multitude of those who had embraced the faith had one heart and one soul, and no one regarded any of their good as their property; on the contrary, they put all great power to mark the testimony given by the apostles to the resurrection of the Lord Jesus, and a great grace worked in them all. No one among them was destitute: indeed, those who had land or houses sold it, brought the price of the goods they had given and deposited it at the apostles' feet. Each received a share of them, according to his needs."em comum. Um

[104] Cf.Matthew 6:33.

[105] I mean, obnoxious, repulsive, obnoxious.

[106] John 4:23 to 24. "But the hour is coming - and it is now - when the true worshippers will worship the Father in spirit and truth, for such are the worshippers the Father seeks. God is spirit, and those who worship Him must worship Him in spirit and truth."

[107] Cf.John 1:18.

[108] Cf. Matthew 18:10. *See* footnote number 49.

[109] Cf. Matthew 5:8.

[110] Cf. Exodus 3:14-15.

111   Genesis 32: "... And one fought with him until the dawn arose. When he saw that he did not subdue him, he touched his thigh joint, and Jacob's thigh dislocated as he wrestled with him. He said, Let me go, for the day has already broken. ' But Jacob answered, I will not leave you unless you bless me. 'He asked him, 'What is your name? ' Jacob replied. He said again, Thou shalt no more be called Jacob: but Israel, because thou hast been strong against God and against men, and hast prevailed. 'Jacob asked this question: «Please reveal your name to me. ' But he answered, «Why do you ask for my name? ' And right there he blessed you. Jacob gave this place the name of Famuel because, he said, 'I saw God face to face and my life was saved'. At sunrise, he had passed Famuel and mannequin of a thigh. So the Israelites, until today, do not eat the sciatic nerve that is in the thigh joint, because He struck Jacob at the thigh joint, at the sciatic nerve." (verses 33)25 a

112   "Verily I say unto you, Among them that are born of women there hath not risen one greater than John the Baptist, and yet he that is least in the kingdom of heaven is greater than he." (Matthew 11:11) This saying of Jesus is corroborated by the gospel of Luke 7:28. The expression "born of woman" means natural birth, not including the birth of the Son of God, who was born in a supernatural way.

113   It is a contradiction to say that Mary is "mother of God", since God the Son pre-existed the creation of the human being; Then how can Mary be the mother of God?

114   BTE, Luke 3:16-17: "I baptize you with water, but he who is stronger than I comes, and I am not saying to untie his sandal

strap. He will baptize you in the Holy Spirit and in the fire; And he hath in his hand the fan, to scatter his threshingfloor, and to gather the wheat into his granary: But he shall burn the refuse in the fire that is not quenched." This passage is corroborated in Matthew 3:11.

[115]   Cf.1 John 4:4.

[116]   Matthew 12:36-37. *See* also footnote number 19 and the corresponding text.

[117]   Colossians 2:16. "Let no man therefore condemn you for food or drink, for a feast, for a new moon, or for sabbaths." (Ecumenical Bible version)

[118]   Mark 2:27: "And he said to them, 'The Sabbath was made for man and not man for the Sabbath, so that the Son of Man is lord even of the Sabbath. '"

[119]   Cf. Luke 14:14-17;

[120]   Matthew 12: "The ears plucked. At that time Jesus happened to pass through a field of wheat on a Sabbath day. His disciples were hungry and began to pluck the ears and eat them. And when the Pharisees saw it, they said unto him, Look unto thy disciples, who do that which they are not permitted to do on the sabbath day. 'He answered them, 'Have you not read what David did, when he was hungry, he and his companions, how he entered the house of God and how they ate the showbread, which neither he nor his companions were allowed to eat, but the priests? '" (verses 1 to 4). Cf. Ecumenical Bible Version.

121   "Or have ye not read in the law, that on the sabbath day in the temple the priests break the sabbath without fault." (Matthew 12:5) Cf. Ecumenical Bible Version.

122   Luke 14. "3. Jesus spoke and said to the coroners and the Pharisees: Is it permissible or not to heal a sick person on the Sabbath day? 4. But they stayed , taking the sick, healed him and dismissed him. 5. And he said unto them, Which of you, if his son or his ox fall into a well, will he not immediately withdraw therefrom on the sabbath day? And they could not object to that." (Ecumenical Bible version)em silêncio. Então Jesus

123   Cf. Luke 13:15.

124   Luke 13: "The ruler of the synagogue, being angry, because Jesus had healed on the Sabbath day, answered and said to the multitude, There are six days to labor. For in those days ye must come to heal, and not on the sabbath day." And the LORD said unto him, O perverse spirits, doth not every one of you unleash out of the manger his ox, or his ass, to cause him to drink on the sabbath day? And this woman, the daughter of Abraham, whom Satan called eighteen years ago, is it not on the Sabbath day that she must be loosed from this yoke? '" (ecumenical Bible version)

125   Cf. Matthew 6:9.

126   "When a man insults his father or his mother, he will be punished with death; He insulted father and mother, his blood falls on him." (Leviticus 20:9)

127   Cf.Matthew 19:5.

128   BTE, 1 Corinthians 11:3-5: "But I want you to know this: the head of every man is Christ: the head of a woman is man; The head of Christ is God. Every man who prays or prophesies with his head covered dishonors his head. But every woman who prays or prophesies with her head uncovered dishonors her head, for it is just as if her head were shaved... Man must not put a veil on his head: he is the image and the glory of God; but the woman is the glory of man."

129   Genesis 3:19: "In the sweat of your face you shall eat your bread until you return to the ground, for you were formed of it: for you are dust, and to dust you shall return."

130   See Psalms 1:1 to 3.

131   Leviticus 18:22: "You shall not lie with a man as one lies with a woman: this would be an abomination." (BTE) The punishment for homosexuals consisted in the death of both men according to Leviticus 20:13.

132   "You shall not have intercourse with the wife of your countryman, and that shall make you unclean." (Leviticus 18:20) Thus, not only the adulteress commits sin, but the man who lies with her. See also Deuteronomy 22:22.

133   According to the extensive relation contained in Leviticus 18:18.

134   "If a young virgin be betrothed to a man, and another man find her in the city, and lie with her, ye shall bring them both unto the gate of the city, and stone them; and they shall die: the young woman because she cried not for help while she was in the city; And the

man, because he hath possessed his neighbour's wife. You will eliminate evil from your midst.

If it be in thy fields that a man shall find the young bride, and shall take her by force, and lie with her; the man that lieth with her shall be the only one to die; thou shalt do nothing unto the young woman: for she hath not committed a sin worthy of death: It is similar to the case of a man who throws himself on his neighbor and kills him: he found her in the field, the young bride cried out, and no one came to his help." (Deuteronomy 22:23-27)

[135] Leviticus 18: "You shall not lie with an animal, which will make you unclean; And no woman shall offer herself to an animal to have intercourse with it: it would be depravity." (verse 23). The penalty for this was the death of the man/woman and the animal according to Leviticus 20:15 and 16.

[136] Cf. Leviticus 19:13.

[137] Leviticus 19: "Do not commit kidnapping, do not lie, do not commit falsehood to the detriment of a compatriot. Utter no false oath under my name; You would desecrate the name of your God. I am the LORD." (verse 11)

[138] Cf. Leviticus 19:27 to 28.

[139] Leviticus 17: "If a man who is a member of the house of Israel or of the migrants who live there consume blood, I will turn against him who has consumed blood, to cut him off from among his people; For the life of a creature is in the blood; And I gave it unto you upon the altar for the absolution of your life. Indeed, blood provides absolution

because it is life. Behold, I said unto the children of Israel, Let none of you consume blood; and let no migrant that dwelleth among you consume blood. '" (verses 12).10 a

140   "Stand up before white hair, and be full of respect for an old man; This is how you shall fear your God. I am the LORD."

141   Cf. Leviticus 19:35.

142   *Indez Steps to a Better Life*, p. 12.

143   Cf. Psalm 15.

144   Cf. Isaiah 33:15.

145   Cf. Micah 6:8.

146   Cf. Habakkuk 2:4.

147   According to what will be addressed in the chapter "Sanctifying Oneself", it is more appropriate to say that the Christian is subject to justice.

148   John 5:39: "You search the Scriptures because you think you have eternal life, and it is they who bear witness to me." (BTE)

149   Matthew 22:29: "Jesus answered them, 'You are in error, for you know neither the Scriptures nor the power of God. '" (BTE)

150   John 14:15: "If you love me, you will keep my commandments." (BTE)

151   By the way, read the chapter "Sanctifying yourself", to deepen the theme.

152   We also know God supernaturally when the Triune God manifests.

[153]   Cf. John 10: "30. I and the Father are one" and Matthew 28: "19. Go ye therefore, and make disciples of all nations, baptizing them in the name of the Father, and of the Son, and of the Holy Ghost, teaching them to observe all that I have commanded you."

[154]   Read: 1) Malachi 3: "I, the Lord, am not changed. Therefore, you descendants of Jacob were not destroyed." 2) Hebrews 13: "8. Jesus Christ is the same, yesterday, today, and for ever." (Bible NIV)

[155]   Proverbs 7: "1. My son, keep my sentences, keep my precepts. 2. Keep my precepts, and live; my instruction be the apple of your eye. 3. Bind it to your fingers, write it on the tablet of your heart..."

[156]   Proverbs 7:1-3, "Keep my words, my son, and lay up my precepts. If you want to live, observe my precepts and my teaching, as the pupil of your eyes. Hold them in your fingers. Write them on the tablet of your heart." (BTE)

[157]   It is also certain that Jesus brought about some changes as will be seen later, which are due to divine mercy.

[158]   The true, biblical God is great, not the God that many believe in in their imagination. Some even believe that the universe was created by God, but doubt that the All-god

-Mighty, creator of the Universe, could have bequeathed to us his Word, just as He wanted it to come to us. These people always have a "but" before biblical truths: the Bible was written by men thousands of years ago, being compiled and translated by many others. I firmly believe that the Bible is the Word of God, written by men of God and inspired by Him, a belief that was based on the experiences I have had in my life. It is a wrong practice to form a "personal Bible", pinching from the Bible some verses - usually promises - and rejecting the rest of the Word. The Word of God is forceful. Often, the Christian does not want to accept the warnings addressed to him.

159   This expression is used by the BTE and means that Jesus did not come to totally repeal the law (abrogate it), but undoubtedly came to modify it in part.

160   The "i" is the smallest letter of the Hebrew and the comma the smallest sign. With this, Jesus demonstrates that the whole Word of God is important and we must apply ourselves to observing it.

161   In Matthew 28:20, Jesus promises, "Behold, I am with you always, even unto the end of the world!"

162   Cf. Luke 18:20-21.

163   Of course, the rich young man was in a unique historical moment: the opportunity to be a follower of God the Son, and it is noticeable that Jesus saw the qualities of the rich young man, as respectful of the Law, when making the invitation.

164   According to several biblical passages. Matthew 9: "Then Jesus went up and crossed the sea again, and came to his city. Behold, they brought him a paralytic lying on a stretcher. Seeing their faith, Jesus said to the paralytic: Trust me, **my son, your sins are forgiven. 'Now some scribes** said to themselves, 'Make this man blaspheme! ' Knowing what they thought, Jesus said: Why have bad thoughts in your hearts? That it is easier? Say: Your sins are forgiven' or say: Get up and walk'? Well done! So that you may know that the Son of Man has authority on earth to forgive

sins' - then he says to the paralytic: get up, take your litter and go home. The man got up and went home. When the multitudes saw this, they were seized with fear, and gave glory to God, who gives such authority to men. (Matthew 9:1 to 8, BTE; the highlight is not in the original text)

165   Matthew 23: "23. Woe unto you, scribes and Pharisees, hypocrites, that pay tithes of mint and fennel and cummin, while neglecting the gravest thing in the law, which is righteousness, and mercy, and truth: This is what needed to be done, without omitting it." (BTE)

166   The penalty was no more than the person who sinned according to Deuteronomy 24:16.

167   In the event of the death of her husband, his brother, fulfilling his duty as a brother-in-law, must take his sister-in-law as his wife. Refusing this, his sister-in-law "shall come to him in the presence of the elders; And she shall take off her sandal from off her foot, and shall spit on her face; Then shall he speak and say, 'This is how it is done to a man who does not rebuild his brother's house! 'And in Israel it shall be called the barefoot house" (Deuteronomy 25:9-10). Note, however, that this is almost an ethical question, since the brother-in-law can refuse to marry his sister-in-law, not a sin, but an ethical duty of the brother-in-law.

168   Deuteronomy 25: "If the culprit deserves to be flogged, the judge will make him lie on the ground and be flogged with a number of blows commensurate with his guilt. No more than forty blows will be struck to prevent your brother from being seriously wounded when he crosses that line and becomes contemptible in your eyes." (verses 2 and 3, BTE)

169   According to Deuteronomy 25:11-12, if the woman strikes a "low blow" to the contender of her man/husband.

170   Cf. Leviticus 20:9.

171   Cf. Matthew 7:1.

172   Luke 17: "3. Be on your guard. Nay. If your brother offends you, rebuke him; And if he repent, forgive him. 4. And if he offend thee seven times a day, and seven times return unto thee, saying, Repent I repent, thou shalt forgive him. '" (BTE)

173   2nd Thessalonians 3: "14. If anyone disobeys what we say in this letter, notice him and I have suspended any relationship with him, that he may be ashamed; But consider him not as an enemy, but correct him as a brother." (BTE) However, this procedure can be badly and arbitrarily used, contrary to the teaching of Jesus contained in the parable of the tares and wheat.

174   Matthew 13: "He told them another parable: The same thing happens with the Kingdom of Heaven as with a man who sowed good seed in his field. While the people slept, their enemy came; He sowed tares on top, right in the middle of the wheat, and went away. When the grass grew and gave ears, then the chaff also appeared. The servants of the master of the house have come to say unto him, Lord, is it not good seed which thou hast sown in thy field? Where then does there come to be tares in it? ' He said to them, An enemy did it. ' The servants said to him, 'So you want us to take it away? No, he said, let it not happen, that you take away the tares, and pluck out the wheat with them. Let them both grow till the harvest, and at the time of the harvest I will say to the reapers: Take the

tares first, and beat them into bundles to burn them; But gather the wheat into my barn. '" (BTE, Matthew 13:24-30)

[175]		John 5: "24. Verily, verily, I say unto you, He that heareth my word, and believeth on him that sent me, hath eternal life; He did not come to judgment, but passed from death to life." (in BTE version)

[176]		Verse 7: "Thou shalt not utter the name of the LORD thy God in vain: for the LORD will not let him go unpunished that uttereth his name in vain."

[177]		Luke 10:29 to 37.

[178]		For the Jew of that time, only the Jew was considered to be the next, not the foreigner according to Exodus 20:16-17; 21:14.18.35; Leviticus 19:11.13.15-18.

[179]		Luke 6:27-28: "But I say to you who hear me, love your enemies, do good to those who hate you, bless those who curse you, pray for those who slander you." (BTE)

[180]		Ob. cit. , p. 839.

[181]		According to the NIV Bible, the Samaritans comprised a "mixed-blooded race, resulting from mixed marriages among the Israelites left behind when the people of the Northern Kingdom were exiled, and the Gentiles brought into the country by the Assyrians (2Rs 17:24). There was acrimonious hostility between the Jews and the Samaritans in the days of Jesus (v. John 4:9)." (note to verse 5 of Matthew 10)

[182]		Regarding the Sabbath, we turn to the chapter: "

The commandments of God refer to avoid repetitions.

[183]   It was consensus among the leaders of the Early Church that the freedom to eat food did not extend to blood.

[184]   Cf. Matthew 5:27.

[185]   Luke 19:20: "And the other came and said, O Lord, behold thy pound, which I have laid upon a handkerchief. 21. For I feared thee, because thou art a severe man, thou takest that which thou hast not laid, and reapest that which thou hast not sown. ' 22. And he said, O wicked servant, I judge thee by thy mouth. You know that I am a strict man, that I take what I have not deposited and reap what I have not sown. 23. Why then did you not entrust my money to the bank. '"

[186]   Cf.Matthew 12:39

[187]   His interpretation of adultery was that sin was consummated by physical act. The Lord Jesus teaches that spiritually it is as serious to look at a woman with an unclean intention as to do the physical act. That kind of reasoning can be applied to homicide, for example. Whoever nourishes, in his heart, a desire to kill his neighbor has a heart and mind as unclean as the murderer who takes his intention to the streets.

[188]   The Mosaic law allowed the husband, soon after marriage, to give a letter of divorce to his wife, repudiating her, if he did not find "more grace in her eyes, because she saw in her something unseemly", according to Deuteronomy 24:1. Now the divorce had been consented to the hardness of the human heart, but the Lord Jesus declared that there is no more sin if the reason for the divorce is fornication according to Matthew 5:32.

189   In accordance with Chapter 21 of Exodus, certain damages committed by a Jew must be repaid for other equivalent or more serious damage. To strike the father or mother was punished with death (verse 15); murder by cunning was punishable by death (verse 14); If the ox is horned, and its owner knows the violence of the ox, and the owner is punished with death (verse 29); The wound with the destruction of the servant's eye resulted in his release (verse 26). The Lord Jesus, however, taught that we should not resist the evil man and turn the other cheek (Matthew 5:38-39). The penalties imposed among the Jews were intended to sanctify the place where God dwelt, eliminating from the people those who were unclean. These precepts lost their purpose, bearing in mind that, from the Lord Jesus, our body became the Temple inhabited by God and it is He who is no longer to be profaned with impurities (negative feelings and thoughts), and no longer the tabernacle and adjacencies.

190   The commandments themselves contain no precept in the sense of hating one's enemies; Instead, in Leviticus 19:17, God commands that one should not hate or hold a grudge. However, some prophets, what could be understood that some writings (prophets), **(?)** lead to think-

There is a lack of love for enemies. The annotation "v" to verse 43, p. 1289, from the Jerusalem Bible mentions the book of Ecclesiasticus 12:4-7 and the writings of Quran (1QS 1:10), which do not make up the Bible adopted by the evangelicals, and the Commentator states that there are in them "such an aversion to sinners that it is not far from hatred, and this is what Jesus might have been thinking".

191   According to John 2: "The Passover of the Jews was at hand, and Jesus went up to Jerusalem. In the Temple he found the sellers of oxen, sheep and doves, as well as the money changers who had settled there. And he made a whip with cords, and cast them all out of the temple, and the sheep, and the oxen; And he spread the money of the money-changers, and overthrew their tables, and said unto the dove-sellers, Take all this away from here, and make not my Father's house a house of business. 'His disciples remembered what was written: «Let the zeal of your house devour me. '". (John 2:13 to 17, BTE)

192   Mark 10: "A few Pharisees come forward and ask him if a man is allowed to put away his wife. He answered them: What did Moses prescribe? ' They said: 'Moses allowed to write a certificate of repudiation and dismiss his wife. 'Jesus said to them, 'It was because of the hardness of your heart that he wrote this commandment for you. But in the beginning of the world God made them male and female; Therefore shall a man leave his father and mother, and bind himself to his wife, and they shall both become one flesh. So they are no longer two, but one flesh. Therefore let not man put asunder what God hath joined together. ' When he was at home, the disciples asked him again about this matter. And he said unto them, If any man put away his wife, and marry another, he is an adulterer concerning the first: And if a woman put away her husband, and marry another, she is an adulteress. '" (Mark 10:1-12, BTE)

193   From this perspective, any criticism of the survival of this Jewish custom is emptied.

194 Acts 10: "10. It was about noon. I was hungry and wanted to eat. As they prepared their food, the open heaven fell and an object, like a large towel held by the four horns, descended to the earth. And within were all the four-footed, and the creeping things, and all the birds of the air. Once I said to him, Get up, Peter, get up and eat. ' But Peter said, No way, Lord! For I have never eaten anything unholy and unclean! ' Again, for the second time, the voice replies, «Do not call what God has declared clean unclean. This was repeated three times. Then the object was gathered up to heaven." (Acts 10:10-16)em êxtase. Via

195 The non-Jews (Gentiles) began to receive the baptism of the Holy Spirit as foreseen in the Holy Scriptures.

196 Acts 15:7 to 11.

197 Ob. cit. , p. 37.

198 Ob. cit. , p. 37.

199 According to Hugo Schlesinger and Humberto Porto, in the work *Jesus was a Jew*, washing hands before prayer or meals was a custom "that was not part neither of the written law nor of the oral tradition". At the time of Jesus, as read (5,13), the custom was condensed in the following formula: "To wash one's hands one's care, but water after meals is obligatory for all." "In hygienic terms, it is explainable, because at the time there were no cutlery or napkin. Anyway, it was not a rabbinical precept; It may even date back to a generation before Jesus. No Pharisee, no matter how quick he was, could be offended by the fact that Jesus' disciples omitted such a habit, as if they were violating the law of Moses. There was no obligation at that point. Mark's record (7:8), according to

which Jesus said that it was a man's tradition, has nothing to do with the divine precepts of the Torah, is historically certain" (p. 131).em Tossefta Beraqchoth

200   Cf. Matthew 15:3 to 7.

201   Colossians 2: "16. Therefore, let no one reproach you for what you eat or drink, or for not celebrating Jewish feasts and holidays, or new moon ceremonies, or Saturdays. 17. These were only temporary precepts, which ended when Christ came."

In the case of the Sabbath, it is not a tradition, but one of the ten commandments to be followed. But the Sabbath was instituted for man, and not man for the Sabbath as the Lord Jesus taught us. As for food and drink, the Son of God purified the food by saying, "It is not that which entereth into the mouth that maketh a man unclean, but that which proceedeth out of the mouth that maketh him unclean." (Matthew 15:11)

202   Exodus 34: "18. You shall keep the feast of unleavened bread. Seven days shalt thou eat unleavened bread, as I commanded thee, at the time appointed in the month of Abib: for in the month of Abib thou camest forth out of Egypt... 22. You shall observe the feast of weeks: the firstfruits of the wheat harvest, and the feast of the harvest at the new year."

203   Genesis 4: "1. The man met Eve, his wife, she conceived and gave birth to Cain, and said, I acquired a man with the help of Iahweh. 2. Then she also bore Abel, Cain's brother. Abel became a shepherd and Cain cultivated the soil."

204   According to Exodus 28:1. "And thou shalt bring unto thee Aaron thy brother, and his sons with him, of the children of Israel; that they may be my priests; Aaron, and Nadab, and Abihu, and Eleazar, and Ithamar, the sons of Aaron. 2. And thou shalt make for Aaron thy brother holy garments for glory and for ornament. 3. Thou shalt say unto all that are wise-hearted, whom I have filled with the spirit of wisdom, that they make garments for Aaron, to consecrate him to the office of the priesthood."

205   "... Thus shall he proceed unto the Tent of Meeting, which abideth with them in the midst of their defilements. No one should be in the Tent of Meeting from the time he enters to make atonement in the sanctuary until he comes out." (Leviticus 16:16-17)

206   "And I will pass through the land of Egypt in that night, and will smite all the firstborn in the land of Egypt, both man and beast; and I, Iahweh, will bring justice upon all the gods of Egypt. But the blood shall be a sign unto you in the houses where ye stand: When I see the blood, I will pass on, and there shall be no scourge of destruction among you, when I smite the land of Egypt." (Exodus 12:12 to 13)

207   Genesis 9: "4. But you shall not eat the flesh alive, that is, its blood. Likewise also of your blood, which is your life, will I require of every beast, and will require a man to give an account: I will require an account of every man for his brother's life." (BTE)

208   Cf. Isaiah 29:13.

209   The version is from the New Life Bible and the highlights are from the Author.

210   Scripture speaks of the "great day of atonement" in Leviticus 16. On that day, the High Priest, who was Aaron, Moses' brother, could carry the blood behind the veil (verse 15).

211   Leviticus 16: "Speak unto Aaron thy brother, that he enter not into the temple at any time, beyond the veil, before the mercy seat which is upon the ark. He may die, for I appear on the mercy seat in a cloud."

212   Cf. Leviticus 16:16.

213   Cf.Matthew 27:51.

214   John 2: "18. The Jews then asked him, saying, 'What sign do you show us to do this? ' 19. Jesus answered them, 'Destroy this temple, and in three days I will raise it up. '"

215   Jesus during a feast of the Jews made an incisive speech about his mission, arguing, "You search the Scriptures because you think you have eternal life in them; Now they are they that bear witness of me." (John 5:39)

216   The Heavenly Council is composed of God (Jehovah), Messiah Jesus Christ, and the Holy Spirit.

217   In the sixth month, the angel Gabriel was sent by God to a city of Galilee called Nazareth, to a virgin betrothed to a man named Joseph, of the house of David, and the virgin's name was Mary. Entering where she was, she said to her: "Rejoice, full of grace, the Lord is with you!" She was intrigued by this word and wondered what the meaning of the greeting would be. But the angel added, "Do not be afraid, Mary! You found grace with God. Behold, thou shalt conceive, and bear a son, and call

his name Jesus. He shall be great, and shall be called the Son of the Most High, and the Lord Yahweh shall give him the throne of David his father: He shall reign in the house of Jacob for ever, and his reign shall have no end." But Mary said to the angel, "How shall this be, if I know no man?" The angel answered, "The Holy Spirit shall come upon thee, and the power of the Most High shall overshadow thee: therefore the holy that is born shall be called the Son of God." (Luke 1:26-35)

218   Chapter 1, verses 5, in the New Life version of the Bible.1 a

219   John 3:19-21: "And this is the judgment: the light came into the world, and men preferred darkness to light, because their works were evil. For every one that doeth evil hateth the light, because his works were evil, lest his works should be exposed. He who acts according to the truth comes to light so that his works may be manifested, since they were done in God."

220   John 5: "In the beginning was the Word and the Word was turned to God, and the Word was God. He was, at first, turned to God. Everything was done through him and without him nothing was done of what was done. In him was life, and the life was the light of men, and the light shineth in darkness, and the darkness understood it not."1 a

221   *Darwin and his Macado.* Editora Vida, 1980. p. 38 to 40.

222   The Old Testament is rich in predictions about the Messiah. Some of these passages: 1) Isaiah 42, where the Lord promises to send his "elect"; Who shall judge the nations, and shall be light unto

them, when he shall take away the prisoner out of the prison, and the inhabitants of darkness out of the prison.

[223] Ob. cit. , p. 120-121.

[224] According to Daniel 7:9-14 in the biblical version adopted by Flusser, ob. cit. , p. 101.

[225] Matthew 1: "17. So the sum of the generations from Abraham to David was fourteen; from David to the exile in Babylon, fourteen; and from the exile in Babylon to Christ, fourteen."

[226] In consonance with Psalm 110:1.

[227] Cf. Luke 7:19, in the Bible version of the Ecumenical Translation.

[228] Cf. Luke 7:22 and 23, in the Bible version of the Ecumenical Translation.

[229] Jesus did not need to flaunt his nature, since the Father bore witness to it through the accomplishment of wonders.

[230] This flight was absolutely necessary because King Herod, though not a Jew, knew the prophecies concerning the Messiah thanks to the advice of wise Israelites and feared the loss of his royal power. Aleksandr Mien describes him as cruel, presumptuous, delusional of grandeur, and, like every usurper, "he was obsessed with suspicion and saw betrayals and conspiracies everywhere" (ob. cit., p. 46 and 47). Regarding the cruelty of Herod, it is enough to mention that he had his wife killed, who was Jewish, and their son, Aristobulus III.

231   King Herod, though not a Jew, was cognizant of the "prophecy surrounding a mysterious Man of Judea who would one day be lord of the whole world," according to Aleksandr Mien, ob. cit. , p. 45.

232   Let it be noted that some scholars ascribe the prophecy to David's reign. David was of the tribe of Judah, according to Psalm 78:68-70. However, the mention of the donkey and the wine seems to evoke the person of Jesus.

233   Acts 2: "23. This man, who was delivered up according to the purpose of God, and the foreknowledge of God, ye delivered him up, crucifying him by the hand of the wicked."

234   Acts 4: "27. Yes, they have indeed joined themselves in this city against your holy servant Jesus whom you anointed. Herod and Pontius Pilate with the heathen nations and the people of Israel, to do all that in thy power, and in thy wisdom, thou hast predetermined."

235   Ob. cit. , p. 48.

236   Ob. cit. , p. 48.

237   In accordance with Aleksandr Mien, in the bibliographical work, p. 36.

238   According to Flusser, in the bibliographical work p. 45.

239   The King of the Jews, Herod, was imposed by Rome; he was not a Jew, but the son of a dignitary of Idumea and a woman of Arabic origin as Aleksadr Mien writes, ob. cit. , p. 46. Interestingly, he married a Jewess of the Hasmonean line, named Alexandra, who were heirs of the royal dynasty that Herod usurped.

240   "Then the Pharisees went out and made a plan, that they might catch him in a trap, and make him speak. They send his disciples to him, with the Herodians, to tell him: «Teacher, we know that you are sincere and teach the ways of God with all truth, without letting yourself be influenced by anyone, for you have no respect for people. So tell us your opinion. Is it permissible to pay tribute to Caesar, yes or no? ' But Jesus, perceiving malice, said: «Hypocrites! Why are you setting me up? Show me the coin that serves to pay the tribute. ' They presented him with the silver coin. He said to them, Whose is this image and inscription? ' They answered, «Caesar's. Then he said to them, Give Caesar what is Caesar's, and God what is God's. ' At these words, they were astonished and, leaving him, withdrew." (Matthew 22:15 to 22, BTE)

241   See that Jesus has well separated spiritual dominion from secular power.

242   Cf. Flusser, ob. cit. , p. 44.

243   The Levites were the Jews who were of the stock of Levi, the son of Jacob, and who were one of the twelve tribes of Israel. The priestly investiture was made by God Himself. Cf. Numbers 8:13 to 16: "Put the Levites before Aaron and before his sons, and present them as an offering given to the Lord. You shall separate the Levites from among the children of Israel, and they shall be mine. After that, the Levites will serve in the meeting tent. Thou shalt therefore cleanse them, and present them as an offering presented. For they are given to me, truly given to me, among the children of Israel: I take them for myself in exchange for all that were born in the first birth, that is, for all the firstborn of the children of Israel."

244		In consonance with the works The Bible: *Literary Introduction, p. 119 and Jesus Master of Nazareth*, p. 35.

245		Cf. Flusser, ob. cit. , p. 49, who cites Josephus as the source.

246		Cf. Flusser, ob. cit. , p. 49.

247		The Pharisees were the ministers of the law to the people, over whom they had great influence and authority, being responsible for the so-called oral tradition. The Sadducees belonged to the priestly aristocracy, but they did not believe in the immortality of the soul and attached importance to the books of the prophets.

248		It is curious that this word means "horse-face", that is, a physiognomy that does not change and can be applied to the human being, as being an inconsistency between thought/feeling and action; a cover-up.

249		Cf. Matthew 23:2.

250		Luke records that Jesus makes mention of love and righteousness, the former being synonymous with the mercy mentioned in Matthew (Luke 11:42).

251		According to Matthew 23: "Woe to you, scribes and hypocritical Pharisees, who pay the tithe of mint and fennel and cumin, while neglecting the gravest thing in the law: righteousness, mercy, and faithfulness; This is what you must do, without omitting it." (verses 23, BTE)

252		"Woe to you, you blind leaders, who say, 'If anyone swears by the sanctuary, it has no value'; But if any man swear by the gold of the sanctuary, he is bound. 'Foolish and blind! What is more important, the gold or the sanctuary that made this gold holy?" (Matthew 23:16-17)

253   "Ye say, If any man swear by the altar, it is of no value, but if any man swear by the offering laid upon it, be bound. 'Blind! What is more important, the offering or the altar that makes this offering sacred? So he that sweareth by the altar sweareth by it, and by all that is upon it; who swears by heaven and swears by the throne of God and by Him who sits on it. " (Matthew 23:18-22)

254   "Woe unto you, written and hypocritical Pharisees, who pay tithes of mint and fennel and cummin, while neglecting the gravest thing in the law: justice, mercy, and truth; This is what was necessary to do, without omitting it." (Matthew 23:23-24)

255   "The Lord said to them, 'Now, you Pharisees, it is the outside of the bowl and dish that you cleanse, but your interior is full of rapacity and wickedness. Fools! Hath not He that made the outward made the inward also? Hence rather in almsgiving that which is within, and then all shall be pure unto you."

256   Luke 11:52: The BTE records that "some ancient witnesses read: *hidden*" instead of "tomastes" (note "t" to article 52).

257   The Pharisees were adherents of the universalization of Judaism, seeking proselytes among the Gentiles.

258   BTE, Matthew 23-15.13 a

259   John 2: "13. The Passover of the Jews was near, and Jesus went up to Jerusalem. 14. In the Temple he found the sellers of oxen and sheep and doves, as well as the money changers who had settled

there. 15. And he made a whip with cords, and cast them all out of the temple, and the sheep, and the oxen; spread the money of the money-changers, overturned their tables; 16. And he said unto the sellers of doves, Take all this hence, and make not my Father's house a house of business. ' His disciples remembered what is written: «The zeal of your house will devour me. '" (Bible in BTE version). The disciples referred to the passage contained in Psalm 69:10.

[260] The Bible teaches us that indignation, or anger, is not a sin, as long as it does not provoke hatred against people. According to Ephesians 4:26 ("when you are angry, do not sin," the NIV Study Bible). Note that the wrath of Jesus was not directed at the Pharisees personally, but at what they were representing. Jesus was indignant at the state of things which the Pharisees helped to build.

[261] Cf. Matthew 23:2.

[262] Cf. Isaiah 53:7.

[263] Matthew 28: "1. After the first day of the week, at first light, Mary Magdalene and the other Mary came to see the tomb. 2. And, behold, there was a great earthquake: for the angel of the Lord descended from heaven, and came near, and rolled back the stone, and sat upon it. 3. And his countenance was like the appearance of lightning, and his raiment white as snow. 4 And the watchmen feared him, and were as dead men. 5. But the Angel, addressing the women, said to them, Do not be afraid! I know that you are looking for Jesus, the crucified one. 6. He is not here, for he is risen, as he said. '"

[264] Cf. Matthew 27:27-50.

265   Matthew 27: "26. He released Barabbas to them. As for Jesus, after he had scourged him, he delivered him up to be crucified."

266   Matthew 27:44: "Even the thieves, who were crucified with him, insulted him."

267   Matthew 27: "57. When even was come, there came a rich man from Arimathea, named Joseph, who also became a disciple of Jesus. 58. And he came to Pilate, and asked him for the body of Jesus. Then Pilate commanded him to be delivered. 59. And Joseph took the body, and wrapped it with a clean sheet 60. and put him in his new tomb, which he had hewn out of the rock. Then rolling a great stone to the entrance of the tomb, he withdrew."

268   Luke 23:24.

269   Matthew 27: "20. But the chief priests and elders persuaded the multitudes to ask for Barabbas, and to destroy Jesus. 21. The governor replied-

-To them: Which of the two would you have me release to you? ' They said, «Barabbas. ' Pilate said, 'What shall I do with Jesus, whom you call the Messiah? ' All answered: Be crucified! ' 23. He said to them again: But what evil has he done? 'But they cried out more vehemently: let him be crucified! ' 24. When Pilate saw that he could do nothing, but rather disorder increased, he took water, and washed his hands in the presence of the multitude, and said, I am innocent of this blood. The responsibility is yours. ' To this all the people answered, Let his blood be on us and on our children. ' 26. Then Barabbas released to them. As for Jesus, after he had scourged him, he delivered him up to be crucified."

270   John 1:36: "When he saw Jesus passing by, he said, 'Behold the Lamb of God. '"

271   We will deal with this matter further in Chapter "Sanctifying Sanctifying

272   "We therefore have an eminent high priest who has crossed the heavens: Jesus, the Son of God. Let us therefore remain firm in the profession of faith. Indeed, we do not have a high priest unable to sympathize with our weaknesses, for he himself was tested in everything like us, except for sin. Let us, then, approach the throne of grace with assurance, so that we may obtain mercy and obtain grace as a timely help.

For every high priest, out of the midst of men, is made for men in their dealings with God. Its function is to offer gifts and sacrifices for sins. He is capable of understanding by those who ignore and err, because he himself is surrounded by weakness. Therefore he must offer sacrifices so much for the sins of the people for his own. Let no man therefore ascribe this honor, save he that is called of God, as Aaron!

In this way, Christ also does not attribute the glory of becoming high priest. But he received it from him who said to him: You are my Son, today I have begotten you... 'It is he who, in the days (?) of his earthly life, presented requests and supplications, with vehement cry and tears, to him who could save him from death; and was met because of his submission. And though he were a son, yet he learned obedience through suffering; And being made perfect, he became to all them that obey him the principle of eternal salvation, having received from God the title of high priest according to the order of Melchizedek." (Hebrews 4:14 to 16; 5:1 to 9)

273   Cf. John 14:6.

274   We have seen that Triune God cannot be reduced to images in Chapter "

The commandments of God, "being evident that one cannot associate God the Son with the serpent, remembering that the serpent was the form that the Evil One assumed in the Garden of Eden. The passage referred to by Jesus is found in Numbers 21: "The people began to criticize God and Moses: read again Why did you bring us up out of Egypt to die in the wilderness? For here is neither bread nor water, and we are clogged up with this food of misery! And the LORD sent fiery serpents against the people, which bit him, and many people died in Israel. ' The people went to Moses, saying: We have sinned by criticizing the LORD and criticizing you: intercede with the LORD to drive away the serpents from us! 'Moses interceded for the people, and the LORD said to him: «Make a fiery serpent, and fasten it on a pole: whosoever is bitten, and looketh upon it, his life shall be saved. Moses made a serpent of brass and fixed it on a pole; And when a serpent bit a man, he looked at the bronze serpent and had his life saved." (Bte, verses 9)5 a

275   "As Moses lifted up the serpent in the wilderness, even so must the Son of Man be lifted up, that whosoever believeth in him should have eternal life."

276   Several biblical passages set in opposition the wisdom of God and the foolishness of the wise men of this world. Thus we find:

"For it was not to baptize that Christ sent me, but to preach the gospel, without resorting to the wisdom of speech, that the cross of Christ should not be made useless. Indeed, the language of the cross is madness for those who are lost, but for those who are saved, for us, it is God's power. For it is written:

I will destroy the wisdom of the wise

And I will destroy the intelligence of the intelligent.

Where is the sage? Where is the learned man?

Where is the writer of this century? Has not God made mad the wisdom of this age? For since the world by wisdom did not recognize God in the wisdom of God, it pleased God by the foolishness of the preaching to save those who believe. The Jews ask for signs, and the Greeks go in search of wisdom; But we preach Christ crucified, which to the Jews is a stumbling-block, to the Gentiles it is foolishness: but to them which are called, both Jews and Greeks, it is Christ, the power of God, and the wisdom of God. For he that is the folly of God is wiser than men, and he that is the weakness of God is stronger than men." (1 Corinthians 1:17:25)

[277] Ob. cit., p. 35.

[278] Cf. Jeremiah 31:31-34 and Hebrews 8:10.

[279] Matthew 27:50: "Then Jesus cried again, and gave up the spirit, and died. 51. Look! At that moment the curtain that separated the Most Holy Place from the Temple was torn from top to bottom; The earth trembled, and the rocks broke."

[280] Cf. John 7:37.

281   Matthew 21: "42. And Jesus asked them, saying, Never have ye read in the scriptures, The stone which the builders rejected, the same is become the chief cornerstone: this is of the Lord, and it is wonderful in our eyes? '" (version VN)

282   Psalm 118: "22. The stone which the builders rejected, that became the chief cornerstone. 23. This is of the Lord, and it is wonderful in our eyes." (version VN)

283   Cf. Romans 5:19.

284   Ob. cit. , p. 79.

285   Cf. 2 [Peter] 1:4.

286   Cf. John 12:24.

287   In Hebrews 2:11, we read, "For both the sanctifier and the sanctified are of one seed: Wherefore is he not ashamed to call them brethren, saying, I will shew thy name unto my brethren; In the midst of the assembly will I praise thee, and more, I will put my trust in him: and further; Behold, I am here with the children whom God hath given me."

288   First [Colossians] 2:11. "When you came to Christ, He delivered you from your evil desires, not through a physical operation of circumcision but through a spiritual operation: the baptism of your souls. 12. In baptism you see how your old sinful nature died with Him and was buried with Him; and then you rose from death with Him to a new life, because you trusted in the Word of the mighty God who raised Christ from the dead. 13. You were dead in sin and your sinful desires had not yet been removed. Then He gave them a share in the very life of Christ, because He forgave them all their sins, 14. and erased the confirmed charges against

you, the list of his commandments which you had not obeyed. Taking this list of sins, He destroyed it by nailing it to the cross of Christ. 15. In this way God took away the power of Satan to accuse you of sin and publicly exhibited to the whole world the triumph of Christ on the cross, where all your sins were taken away."

[289]   Cf. John 4:24.

[290]   Cf. Matthew 23:24.

[291]   Read, by the way, what we defend about intellectual autonomy as opposed to free will.

[292]   Cf. John 4:24: "Verily, verily, I say unto you, He that heareth my word, and believeth on him that sent me, hath eternal life; He does not come to judgment, but has passed from death to life."

[293]   As, for example, in the parable of the mines (Luke 19:13).

[294]   Cf. Genesis 22:12.

[295]   Cf. Genesis 18:16-17: "Jacob woke up from sleep and exclaimed: Truly, it is the LORD who is here and I did not know it! He was afraid and exclaimed: How terrible this place is! It is God's own house, the gate of heaven. '"

[296]   Cf. Genesis 42:17-18: "He imprisoned them all for three days. On the third day Joseph said to them: This is what you will do to stay alive. As for me, I fear God. '"

[297]   Cf. Job 1:1.

[298]   It is the theory that presupposes the existence of a highly intelligent and powerful Being, who created life and all things.

299   Ob. cit. , p. 9.

300   Transgenics are obtained by crossing between two different species of plant or animal origin. We are not giving our opinion on transgenics, but only reporting that the comment that we care about here has come from a report on it.

301   BTE, Isaiah 64:7: "Yet, Lord, you are our Father; We are the clay, and you who model us; We are all the work of your hand."

302   Cf. Isaiah 55:11.

303   John 5:36-40: "Now I have a testimony that is greater than that of John: it is the works that my Father has given me to do, that I do, and that they bear witness concerning me that the Father has sent me. The Father, who sent me, himself testified about me. But ye have not hearkened unto his voice, nor seen that it shewed; and his word remaineth not in you, because ye believe not him that sent me. You persecute the Scriptures because you think that eternal life is acquired by them, and it is they who bear witness to me, but you do not want to come to me to have eternal life."

304   John 14: "6. Jesus says to him: I am the Way, the Truth and the Life. No one comes to the Father except through me. 7.If you know me, you will also know my Father. From this time you have known and seen him. '"

305   Cf. Acts 4:12 and Philippians 2:9.

306   Cf. BTE, Matthew 21:42: "Jesus said to them, Have you never read in the Scriptures: the stone which the builders rejected was the

one which became the cornerstone; This is the Lord's work, admirable thing for our eyes'?".

307   Hebrews 9:27-28: "And as the destiny of men is to die only once - after which comes the judgment -, so Christ was offered once to take away the sins of the multitude..." The passage of Jesus' encounter with Nicodemus (John 3:21) also buries any argument for reincarnation.

308   Cf. BTE, Mark 15:38 and 39: "The veil of the Sanctuary was rent in two parts from top to bottom. The centurion standing in front of him, seeing that he had died thus, said: Truly, this man was the Son of God".

309   Luke 12:8 and 9, Bte: "I say to you: Whoever declares himself for me before men, the Son of Man will also declare himself for him before the angels of God. But he that hath disowned me before men shall be disowned before the angels of God."

310   Cf. BTE, John 10:14: "I am the good shepherd, I know my sheep, and my sheep know me, as my Father knows me, and I know my Father, and I lay down my life for the sheep."

311   Psalm 23: "Iahweh is my shepherd, I lack nothing. 2. In green pastures he maketh me to lie down. He leadeth me unto still waters, and restoreth my strength: He leadeth me in good ways for his name's sake. 4. Though I walk through a valley of the shadow of death, no evil will I fear; for he is with me: Thy rod and thy staff leave me at ease."

312   "Whosoever of you hath a friend, and goeth to seek him in the middle of the night, saying, Lend me three loaves of bread,

O my friend; for one of my friends is come from a journey, and I have nothing to offer him' and he shall answer from within, saying, Trouble me not: The door is already shut, and my children and I are in bed; I can't get up to give them to you'; I tell you, even if he doesn't get up to give them for being a friend, he will stand up at least because of their insistence, and give him everything he needs." (Luke 11:5 to 8)

[313]   Luke 14:16 to 24.

[314]   Cf.Luke 14:24.

[315]   G. C. Berkouwer. *Biblical Doctrine of Sin.* Editora Aste, São Paulo, 1970.

[316]   He also told the following parable to some who were convinced of being righteous and despised all others: "Two men went up to the Temple to pray; One was a Pharisee and the other a tax collector. The Pharisee stood and prayed thus with himself: «O God, I thank You that You are not like other men, who are thieves, evildoers, adulterers, or even like this tax collector. I fast twice a week, I tithe everything I get. 'The tax collector, keeping himself at a distance, did not even want to lift his eyes to heaven, but beat his breast, saying, 'God has compassion on the sinner that I am! 'I say unto you, He went down to the justified house, but not the other; for every man that rises shall be brought down, but he that stoops shall be raised up." (Luke 18:9 to 14, BTE version)

[317]   Cf. Leviticus 16:40-42, in the BTE version.

[318]   Cf. Job 1:1, version of the BTE.

[319]   Why doesn't the Almighty set deadlines?

Why can't your faithful see your days?

Move the landmarks of the land, lead to pasture herds surrupiados;

The ass that is fatherless is carried away: the ox that is the widow's is taken for a pledge.

The destitute are thrown out of the way, all the poor of the earth must hide.

Like wild donkeys in the desert

They leave early for work, in search of food;

It's the heat that feeds your children.

In the fields they cut for themselves some forage, they search the vineyard of the bad.

Because they lack clothes, they spend the night naked and, against the cold, they have no cover.

They are soaked in the rain of the mountains and, having no shelter, narrow the rocks.

You rip the little orphan out of his breast and make a pledge to the poor.

They tell him to walk around naked, leaving him no clothes;

The hungry are ordered to carry the bundles.

In the place of others they will squeeze oil, and those who tread the winepress thirst.

[320] Cf. Job 40:3 to 5, version of the Bible. Ecumenical Translation.

[321] Matthew 11:28 to 30.

[322] Cf.1a [John] 1:9.

[323] Paulus Publishing, p. 75.

324   Cf. BTE, Matthew 26:27: "Then he took a cup, and when he had given thanks, he gave it to them, saying: 'Drink of it all, for this is my blood, the blood of the covenant, shed for the multitude, for the forgiveness of sins'."

325   Cf. BTE, John 8:34: "Jesus answered them: Verily, verily, I say unto you, He that committeth sin is the servant of sin. The slave does not always remain in each; But the son abideth therein for ever. If, therefore, it is the Son who frees you, you will really be free'."

326   Cf. BTE, Galatians 2:19: "For I died to the law through the law, that I might live unto God. With Christ I am crucified: I live, but it is no longer I, it is Christ who lives in me. For my life present in the flesh I live by faith in the Son of God, who loved me and gave himself up for me".

327   São Paulo: Editora Fiel Ltda., 1979, p. 8 and 9.

328   "But now, apart from the Law, the righteousness of God is manifested, witnessed by the Law and the Prophets, the righteousness of God working by faith , for all who believe - for there is no difference, Since all have sinned and are deprived of the glory of God - they are justified freely by his grace by virtue of the redemption accomplished : God has set him out as an instrument of propitiation, by his own blood, through faith. He would thus manifest his righteousness, by the fact that he left the sins of old unpunished in the time of God's patience; He wanted to manifest his righteousness at the present time to prove himself righteous and to justify what is by faith, then the reason for glory? You are excluded. In force of what law? The one with the construction? By no means, but in the power of

the law of faith. For we hold that a man is justified by faith, without the works of the law. 29. Or is he the God of the Jews only? It is not also of the Gentiles. Of course also of the Gentiles, for there is only one God, who will justify the circumcised by faith and also the uncircumcised through faith. 31. Do we then eliminate the Law through faith? Not at all! On the contrary, we consolidate it." (Romans 3:28-31)em Jesus Cristoem Cristo Jesusem Jesus. Onde

329   Having therefore been justified by faith, we are at peace with God through our Lord Jesus Christ, by whom we have access by faith to this grace, wherein we stand, and rejoice in the hope of the glory of God.

330   See note 326 below.

331   Cf.John 19:30.

332   Cf. Note 326.

333   Matthew 7: "3. Why notice the speck that is in your brother's eye when you do not see the beam that is in yours? 4. Or how can you say to your brother, 'Let me take the speck out of your eye,' how much you have a beam in yours? Thou hypocrite, take first the beam out of thine eye, and then thou shalt see well, to remove the speck out of thy brother's eye."

334   Matthew 7: "1. Judge not, lest ye be judged. 2. For by the judgment wherewith ye judge ye shall be judged, and by the measure wherewith ye measure ye shall be measured."

335   John 10:10-11

336   Luke 21: "18. But not one hair of your head shall be lost."

337   Matthew 17: "19. Then the disciples, seeking Jesus alone, said, Why could we not cast him out? 'Jesus answered them, 'Because of the weakness of your faith: if you have faith like a mustard seed, you will say to this mountain, 'Carry yourself from here to there, and it will be transported, and nothing will be impossible for you. '"

338   Cf. Ephesians 6:12.

339   Philippians 4: "6. Do not worry about anything; but present to God all your needs by prayer and supplication, in thanksgiving. 7. Then the peace of God, which surpasses all understanding, will guard your hearts and thoughts in Christ Jesus."

340   Mark 2: "1. Being at Capernaum again, after a few days they knew that he was there were so many who gathered that there was no place at the door. And he preached the word unto them. They came to bring you a paralytic, carried by four men. And when they could not draw near because of the crowd, they opened the ceiling to the place where he was, and having made a hole, they lowered the bed on which the paralytic lay: Son, your sins are forgiven. 'Now some of the scribes sitting there reflected in their hearts, 'Why are you talking like that? He is a blasphemer! Who can forgive sins other than the one God? 'Jesus immediately realized what they were thinking in their hearts, and said, 'Why do you think so in your hearts? What is easier to say to the paralytic: your sins are forgiven, or to say, Arise, take up your bed and walk? Well, that you may know that the Son of Man has power to forgive sins on earth, I

command you - he said to the paralytic - to arise, take up your bed, and go to your house. 'The paralytic got up and immediately, carrying the bed, went out before them all, so that they were amazed and glorified God saying, 'We have never seen anything like it! '"em casa. E

341   Acts 17: "10. The brothers immediately made Paul and Silas leave for Berea by night. Having arrived there, they appeared to the synagogue of the Jews. Now their sentiments were nobler than those of Thessalonica. They took the floor with the utmost commitment. Each day they searched the Scriptures to see if everything was accurate. 12. Many of them thus embraced the faith, as well as of the Greeks, ladies of distinction and many men."

342   Cf. Matthew 7:13 and Luke 13:24.

343 Cf. Acts 16:37 and 22:25.

344   The apostle Judas writes of the rebuke to Satan: "8. Now they act in the same way: in their hallucination they defile the flesh, despise Authority and injure the heavenly Dignities. 9. And yet the archangel Michael, when disputing with the devil about the body of Moses, dared not pronounce an injurious sentence against him, but confined himself to saying: The Lord rebukes you! '

Judas (not Iscariot) was referring to the passage located in Zechariah 3: "2. The Angel of Iahweh said to Satan, That Iahweh represses you, Satan, repress Iahweh, who elected Jerusalem."

345   The believer receives the authority of Jesus to cast demons into the abyss. Demons must submit to the authority of God. Demons can be cast into the abyss. Therefore, the demons that possessed

the two Gadarenes cried out, "What is it between us and you, Son of God? Have you come to torment us before the time?" (Matthew 8:29) To escape the abyss, they asked Jesus to cast them into a rod of pigs (verses 30 and 31). However, there is a demonological hierarchy and not all dark ones can be thrown into the abyss immediately.

346   The beloved apostle is John. In 1 John 4:4, we read, "You, little children, belong to God and you have overcome them. For that which is in you is greater than that which is in the world."

347   Cf. Matthew 21:22, in the Bible's version of NIV Studies.

348   "Enter through the narrow gate. Wide is the gate, and broad is the way that leadeth to destruction, and many that enter in by it: How narrow is the gate and narrow is the way that leads to life, and few are the ones who find it." (Matthew 7:13 and 14, Bible version Ecumenical Translation)

349   It reads in 2:19, "Do you believe that God is one? You do well. Demons also believe and tremble."

350   Quote taken from the Great *Laroussecultural Encyclopedia*.

351   BTE, Romans 1:22 and 25: "Pretending to be wise, they became fools, exchanged the glory of the incorruptible God for images that represent corruptible man, birds, quadrupeds, reptiles." "They exchanged the truth of God for a lie, worshipped and served the creature in the place of the Creator." In this sense, also 1 Corinthians 6:10; 1st. Corinthians 10:1; Galatians 5:19.

352   Cf. Romans 2:21.

353   Cf Romans 2:21, Romans 13:9, 1. Corinthians 6:10.

354   Cf. Romans 6:7.

355   Cf. Romans 13:9.

356   Cf. Romans 1:29-30; Romans 13:9; Timothy 1:9.

357   BTE, Ephesians 6:1: "Children, obey your parents in the Lord, this is what is right. Honor your father and mother, it is the first commandment accompanied by a promise: that you may have happiness and long life on earth."

358   Cf. Timothy 1:10.

359   Cf. Romans 13:9.

360   Pentateuch are the first five books of the Bible (Genesis, Exodus, Leviticus, and Deuteronomy).

361   Cf. Galatians 5:19.

362   "Therefore God gave them over to degrading passions: their wives changed their relations against nature; Men likewise, forsaking natural relations with the woman, burned with desire for one another, committing the infamy of man to man, and receiving in his person the just wages of his transgression." (BTE, Romans 1:26-27)

363   Cf. Romans 1:29-30; 2nd. Timothy 3:2.

364   Cf. 1 Corinthians 5:1. This sin was predicted in Leviticus 18:8.

365   Cf. 1 Corinthians 6:15 and 16.

366   Cf. Corinthians 6:10.

367   Cf. 1 Corinthians 6:18-20 (BTE): "Flee from debauchery. Any other sin committed by man is external to his body. But a fornicator sins against his own body. Do you not know that your body is the temple of the Holy Spirit who is in you and who comes from God, and that you do not belong?" See also Ephesians 5:4 and Colossians 3:5.

368   Cf. Galatians 5:19; Timothy 1:10.

369   Cf. Colossians 3:9; Timothy 1:10.

370   Cf. Galatians 5:19.

371   Cf. Galatians 5:19.

372   Cf. Galatians 5:19.

373   Cf. Galatians 5:19.

374 Cf. Galatians 5:19.

375   Cf. Galatians 5:19.

376   Cf. 2 Timothy 3:2.

377   Cf. Ephesians 5:3: "Whoredom, uncleanness, whatever it may be, do not even mention yourselves among yourselves, as is fitting for saints." Also cf. Colossians 3:5.

378   Also cf. Galatians 5:19.

379   According to Timothy 1:10.

380   Also cf. Galatians 5:19 and Ephesians 5:18.

381   Cf. Colossians 3:8.

382   Cf. Timothy 1:10.

383   Cf. 1 Corinthians 7: 1 and 8.

384   Cf. Romans 5:9 to 11.

385   Cf. 2 Thessalonians 3:6.

[386] Cf. Romans 1:24.

[387] Here the word is not used pejoratively. Jesus had already recognized that the Pharisees were sitting on the chair of Moses,

[388] BTE, Philippians 3:4-6: "Nevertheless, I have reason to have confidence in myself also. If any man believe that he can trust himself, him can I, circumcised the eighth day, of the race of Israel, of the tribe of Benjamin, the Hebrew, the son of the Hebrews, concerning the law, the Pharisee, concerning the zeal, the persecutor of the Church: concerning the righteousness which is found in the law, made irreproachable."

[389] Gamaliel, according to Aleksandr Mien, ob. cit., p. 132, was the grandson of the great Rabbi Hilel.

[390] Cf. Acts 22:3 and Acts 5:34.

[391] BTE, Acts 26:10-11: "This is what I did in Jerusalem: I personally imprisoned a great number of saints by virtue of the power which I had received from the chief priests, and I gave my suffrage when they were slain. As I went through all the synagogues, I multiplied my abuse against them, to force them to blaspheme: and in the height of my wrath I persecuted them even unto foreign cities."

[392] Matthew 28:18. "... all authority was given to me in heaven and on earth."

[393] Said the Lord, "... I will have mercy on whom I will have mercy, and I will have compassion on whom I will have compassion." (Exodus 33, verse 19, second part, in the Bible, NIV)

[394] Cf. Matthew 23:23 and Luke 11:42.

395   "...and the LORD repented that he had made man upon the earth. And he was grieved, and said, I will blot out from the face of the ground man whom I have made, man, and great beasts, and small beasts, and even the birds of the air: for I repent that I have made them. But Noah found grace in the eyes of the LORD (Genesis 6:6-8).

396   Moses said to Yahweh, "You said to me, Bring up this people, but you have not revealed to me who you shall send with me. Yet you said, I know you by name, and you have found grace in your sight: and consider that this nation is your people." (Exodus 32:12, Jerusalem Bible)

397   This does not seem to have occurred with the criminal who was crucified to the left of Jesus.

398   Cf. John 15.

399   The BTE brings the following note: "r. The Jews understood well that it was the freedom lived in a relationship with God (politically they were often enslaved); but this freedom is a gift of God and it must be lived in faith..."

400   Cf. Aleksandr Mien: ob. cit. , p. 132, footnote number 5, "the Aramaic word ruach, *as* well *as* its Greek correspondent pneuma, designates both "the wind" and the "spirit".

401   "For by baptism, we were buried with him in his death, that just as Christ was raised from the dead by the glory of the Father, so we also might lead a new life." (Bte, Romans 6:4)

402   "Nicodemus said to him, How could a man be born when he was old? Could he enter a second time into his mother's

bosom and be born? 'Jesus answered him, Verily, verily, I say unto thee, Except a man be born of water and of the Spirit, he cannot enter into the kingdom of God. That which is born of the flesh is flesh, and that which is born of the Spirit is Spirit. '" (John 3:6, BTE version)3 a

[403]   Cf. John 6:51.

[404]   Cf. John 7:38.

[405]   Cf. Matthew 28:20.

[406]   Cf. 1 Colossians 1:18.

[407]   Cf. John 15:1 and John 15:5.

[408]   Cf. 1 Corinthians 1:31.

[409]   Philippians 2:13 (BTE): "For it is God who works in you to will and to do according to his benevolent plan."

[410]   Cf. Philippians 2:13.

[411]   Romans 7: "So I would not have known lust if the law had not said, Thou shalt not covet. Taking advantage of the occasion, sin produced in me all kinds of lusts through the commandment. For without law, sin is a dead thing. Once, in the absence of law, I lived. But the commandment came, sin took life, and I died: the commandment, which must lead to life, proved to me a factor of death. For sin, availing itself of the occasion, seduced me through it, caused my death. So then the law is holy, and the commandment holy and just and good."

[412]   Cf. Romans 7:7 and 12.

[413]   For I know that in me - I mean in my flesh - good does not inhabit: to will the good is within my grasp, but not to do it, since I do not do the good that I want, and do the evil that I do not want. Now if I

do that which I will not, it is not I that act, but sin that dwelleth, that I will

do good, I perceive therefore this law: it is evil within my power. For I delight

in the law of God as an inward man, but in my members I find another law,

which my understanding ratifies: It makes me the prisoner of the law of sin

which is in my members (Romans 7:18-23). This second indication of the

origin of sin is in accordance with the teachings of Jesus according to John

3:6.em mim. Eu

[414]   Cf. Romans 3:23.

[415]   Cf. Galatians 5: "But these are the fruits of the

Spirit: love, joy, peace, patience, goodness, benevolence, faith, sweetness,

self-control, against such things there is no law. Those who belong to Christ

crucified the flesh with its passions and desires. If we live by the Spirit, let

us also walk under the impulse of the Spirit."

[416]   Cf. Matthew 3:10.

[417]   This is what can be drawn from the following

passages: "Now we know that whatever the law says, it says to those who

are under the law, so that every mouth may be closed and the whole world

may be found guilty before God. For this cause shall no man be justified

before Him by the works of the law: Indeed, the law gives only the

knowledge of sin." (Romans 3:19 and 20 Bte)

[418]   The gospels record this revelation on two

occasions: 1) "Verily, verily, I say unto you, he that heareth my word, and

believeth him that sent me, hath eternal life, and cometh not into

judgment, but is passed from death unto life" (John 5:24 - Jerusalem Bible);

2nd) "For the Son of Man will come with his angels in the glory of his Father;

And then shall he render to every man according to his manner" (Matthew 16:27, BTE).

[419]   "Verily, verily, I say unto you, He that heareth my word, and believeth on him that sent me, hath eternal life, and is not in judgment, but is passed from death unto life." (John 5:24 - Jerusalem Bible)

[420]   "For the Son of man shall come with his angels in the glory of his Father; And then he shall render to every man according to his manner." (Matthew 16:27, BTE)

[421]   Cf. Romans 2:6

[422]   "For the Son of man shall come with his angels in the glory of his Father; And then he shall render to every man according to his manner." (Matthew 16:27, BTE)

[423]   Santiago Dantas includes coercibility as an immanent characteristic of the legal norm. He writes: "So, for example, this rule: everyone who insults, everyone who is wronged, from the moment he responds with gesture or in words, becomes even. This rule, which is part of the Code of Chivalry in force in more or less all nations, is not, however, a legal rule, although it serves to compose conflicts of interest and is not a legal rule, for one reason: that if one wants to avoid the action of it, it can always do so, whereas a legal rule has even coerciveness as its characteristic, which means that, if one wants to avoid the action of the legal rule, there is an authority capable of imposing either compliance with the standard, or compliance with an equivalent standard; or it is the rule itself that is fulfilled or else it disappears and another one arises that the State is in a position to impose." (ob. cit., p. 39 and 40)

424 "Know ye not that your bodies are members of Christ?"... "Or do you not know that your body is the temple of the Holy Spirit who is in you and who comes from God, and that you are not your own?"

425 The Church of Christ comprises all the faithful who remain in his Word, regardless of the Christian denomination to which they belong.

426 *Apud* Norman Vincent Peale, ob. cit. , p. 198.

427 BNVI: "Brood of vipers, how can you, who are evil, say good things? For the mouth speaks of that which is full of the heart. A good man out of his good treasure bringeth forth good things: and an evil man out of his evil treasure bringeth forth evil things."

428 Saint Peter quoted the Scriptures: "For he who wants to love life and see happy days must keep the tongue of evil and the lips of deceitful words, turn away from evil and do good, and seek peace, but persecute it." (BTE, 1 Peter 3:10)

429 BTE, John 5: "22. For the Father judges no one, but has committed all judgment to the Son, that all may honor the Son, as they honor the Father. Whoever does not honor the Son does not honor the Father who sent him."

430 BNVI, Exodus 16:35: "The Israelites ate manna for forty years, until they came to a habitable land; ate manna till they reached the borders of Canaan."

431 *Ino Power of Positive Thought*, pp. 142 and 143.

432   Psalm 37: "5. Commit your way to Iahweh, trust in him, and he will act; will manifest your righteousness as light and your right as noon."

433   Cf. Matthew 6:22.

434   Cf. Luke 19:11 to 27 in the BTE.

435   Cf. note "x" to verse 31 of chapter 29, 2nd Chronicle, Ecumenical Bible Translation, p. 1521.

436   BTE: Numbers 25:11 to 13: "Pinhas the priest, the son of Eleazar, the son of Aaron, turned away my wrath from the children of Israel, showing himself jealous in my place. That is why I did not exterminate the children of Israel under the blows of my jealousy. Therefore say unto him, I give him my covenant for peace. It will be for him and his descendants. This covenant will guarantee him the priesthood forever, since he was jealous for his God and performed the rite of absolution for the children of Israel."

437   BTE, Matthew 25:31 to 40: "**The Judgment.** When the Son of Man comes in his glory accompanied by all the angels, then he will sit on his throne of glory. Before him shall all nations be gathered together, and he shall separate men one from another, as a shepherd separates the sheep from the goats. He will place the sheep on his right and the goats on his left. Then shall the king say unto them on his right hand, Come, ye blessed of my Father, I will inherit the kingdom prepared for you from the foundation of the world. Because I was hungry and you fed me; I was thirsty and you gave me drink; I was a stranger and you took me in; I was naked, and ye clothed me; sick, and visited me; in prison, and you came to me. 'Then the righteous will answer him: Lord, when did it happen to us to see you hungry and to feed you, to thirst and to give you drink? When did it happen to us to see you sick or in prison and come to you? And the king shall say unto them, Verily I say unto you, As

often as ye have done it unto one of these least, which are my brethren, ye have done it unto me. '"

438   John 1:45 to 49: "Philip met Nathanael and said to him: «We have found the one of whom Moses wrote in the Law and the prophets: Jesus, the son of Joseph, of Nazareth. 'Nathanael asked him, 'Can something good come out of Nazareth? ' - Come and see,' Philip replied. Jesus saw Nathanael approaching and said of him, «Behold an Israelite indeed, in whom is no pretense. 'Where do you know me? 'Nathanael asked him. - Before Philip called you,' Jesus answered, I saw you, when you were under the fig tree. 'Then Nathanael exclaimed, 'Rabbi, you are the Son of God, you are the King of Israel. 'Jesus answered, 'Believe, just because I said to you, 'Did I see you under the fig tree? You'll see bigger things than this. 'And said unto them, Verily, verily, I say unto you, Ye shall see heaven opened, and the angels of God ascending and descending upon the Son of man. '"

439   Cf. 1 Corinthians 3:16.

440   "The LORD intervened for Sarah, as he had said: He dealt with her according to his word. She became pregnant, gave Abraham a son in his old age, at the time God had told her. Abraham named his son Isaac, whom Sarah had begotten for him" (BTE, Genesis 21:1 to 3).

441   Cf. Genesis 22.

442   "And when they came to the place which God had appointed him, Abraham set up an altar there, and set the logs of wood. He tied his son Isaac up and put him on the wood. Abraham reached out to grab the cleaver and kill his son. Then the angel of the LORD called out from

heaven and cried out, O Abraham! Abraham! ' He answered, I am here. ' He continued: Don't stretch out your hand against the young man. Do nothing to him, for now I know that you fear God, you who have not spared your son, your only son, for me. '" (Bte, Genesis 22:9 to 12)

443   Cf. Genesis 22:8.

444   *In Oremos,* p. 56.

445   Cf. Luke 10:2.

446   Cf. BTE, Matthew 10:34-35: "Do not imagine that I have come to bring peace on earth; I have not come to bring peace, but the sword. Yes, I have come to separate the man from his father, the daughter of his mother, the daughter-in-law from his mother-in-law; Someone's enemies will be the people in their own home."

447   Luke 21: "19. It is by perseverance that you will maintain your lives."

448   "Thomas says to him, Lord, we do not know where you are going. How can we know the way? ' Jesus says to him: I am the Way, the Truth and the Life, no one comes to the Father except through me. If you know me, you will also know my Father. Henceforth ye know him, and have seen him." (John 14:5-7)

449   Paul compared athletes to Christians. Athletes train with great dedication and discipline and abstain from many things, but they seek a perishable prize. Christians, likewise, must obtain training and discipline through the Word of God, but the prize we aim for is incorruptible. Try to read I Corinthians 9:25 and II Timothy 2:5.

450   Cf. John 6:37 to 40.